Special Delivery

Special Delivery

Edited by Sarah Goldstein

TARGUM/FELDHEIM

First published 2004
Copyright © 2004 by Sarah Goldstein
ISBN 1-56871-311-8

All rights reserved

No part of this publication may be translated, reproduced, stored in a retrieval system, or transmitted in any form or by any means, electronic, mechanical, photocopying, recording, or otherwise, without prior permission in writing from both the copyright holder and the publisher.

Published by:
TARGUM PRESS, INC.
22700 W. Eleven Mile Rd.
Southfield, MI 48034
E-mail: targum@netvision.net.il
Fax: 888-298-9992
www.targum.com

Distributed by:
FELDHEIM PUBLISHERS
202 Airport Executive Park
Nanuet, NY 10954
www.feldheim.com

Printing plates by "Frank," Jerusalem

Printed in Israel

*In loving memory of
Marilyn Goldstein
forever inspiring those around her
who passed away on
18 Tishrei 5764 (October 14, 2003)*

*Eternally remembered
by her husband Sidney
her children Nancy, David, and Alice
and their families*

*With everlasting hakaras hatov to the Ribbono shel olam for entrusting us with His precious and treasured jewels —
our children and grandchildren.
May we be worthy of them.*

May He shower His blessings upon Sarah Goldstein as she does her avodas hakodesh and helps to bring future Yiddishe neshamos into this world.

Shmuel and Rochel Rochkind

The stories in this book are not meant to be taken as medical advice. Any medical information contained therein was added to clarify the story and cannot be used as a general rule. Even if your situation appears similar, a competent caregiver must be consulted.

Some of the names in the stories have been changed to protect privacy. The stories, however, are accurate.

Contents

Acknowledgments 11
Foreword 13
Introduction 15
Strength through Emunah 19
Baby Building 23
They Will Turn. 27
Over Forty-five. 32
Birth Surprise in Jerusalem 37
My Cesarean Birth Experience 42
Taxi Baby. 45
Day by Day. 51
Wheelchair Birth. 54
When the Unexpected Occurs… 57
Don't Overorganize 63
There's No Place Like Home 65
Mensch Tracht und Gott Lacht. 71

Sterile Scissors	76
My VBAC Birth Adventure	79
The Ambulance That Almost Made It	84
In Joy I Reap	87
Ladies' Room Birth	98
No Surprises, Please!	100
In for a Landing	109
Two Sisters, Two Births	115
Birth Center Birth	123
A Beacon in the Fog	128
Jacuzzi Birth	131
The Next Best Thing	135
Postpartum's Gaping Black Hole	138
Snowstorm over Jerusalem	146
It's a Girl!	150
Afterword	157
Glossary	159
Glossary of Medical Terms	163

Acknowledgments

Although they seem few, the following people did more than the normal share to help this book develop.

Thank you to all the doctors, midwives, and experienced labor coaches who put up with me on the phone or in the delivery room. It's taken six years and various conferences and lectures to reach the point where I know I have much more to learn. I thank you all for your patience.

All the women I have helped: thank you for your confidence in my ability to bring out your physical and emotional strengths and allowing me to help you birth your babies.

To Mrs. Masha Fabian, certified ASPO-Lamaze childbirth educator, who had confidence that my skills would get even sharper.

To Henci Goer, author of *Obstetric Myths versus Research Realities* and *The Thinking Woman's Guide to a Better Birth*, for her long-distance advice and guidance. Hooray for e-mail!

To Michal Finkelstein, author of *B'Sha'ah Tovah* and *The Third Key* and my friend of twenty-three years, whose connection with me became closer when both our paths led us to Israel and even more so when I became a doula.

To Meir Zarovsky, photographer and longtime friend, whose creativity helped put the finishing touches on the cover.

Suri Brand, a neighbor and friend who, in all those capacities as well as a Targum proofreader, has helped to take this book from beginning to end.

The staff at Targum Press, especially Rabbi Dombey, who had the patience to explain to me three times how to cut and paste (on a computer).

My children, who put up with days and many nights of phones ringing, people at the door, and their mom not always there when they needed her. Thanks for your dedication to the cause of helping birthing women everywhere, even when the "B word" became impossible to bear.

And my husband, who assisted with everything from how to put an idea on paper to replenishing the fax paper. I hope one day he will catch up on those sleepless nights.

Foreword

By Michal Finkelstein

Giving birth is never a commonplace event. No matter where a woman delivers a child, whether it be in a hospital, at home, or in transit, childbirth is a miracle. As a midwife, I would often be asked, "Don't you love delivering babies?" But I never considered the midwife or the doctor the one who delivers babies. It is the woman herself.

Every laboring woman has the power to bring forth new life. The midwives, doctors, coaches, and husbands are there only for support. Hashem blessed women with incredible spiritual and physical strength to further His will in this world by giving birth. We rejoice in this special relationship with our Creator, and our hearts swell with pride at every opportunity to strengthen our connection with Him — and childbirth is one of the most intimate and intense parts of that relationship.

During our friendship of over twenty years, Sarah has displayed the characteristics of honesty, loyalty, and devotion to her family, friends, and community. She has dedicated herself to the promotion of childbirth education and support of birthing women in the city of Jerusalem. Not only that, she has spent many hours trying to raise the level of awareness of childbearing women concerning the importance of childbirth education and the availability of knowledgeable and helpful doulas. She has instituted a program to raise the educational levels of doulas in the community and, on her own initiative, has acted as a liaison between community doulas and the hospitals in Jerusalem.

In this book, Sarah Goldstein has given us a look at the power of women experiencing birth in many different circumstances. We witness how faith in God, family, and friends turn difficult moments into positive experiences. Though my personal approach to childbirth may be different from some of the examples in this book, we can all learn from these brave and creative women.

Thank you, Sarah.

Michal Finkelstein, RN, CNM
Author of *B'Sha'ah Tovah*
and *The Third Key* (soon to be published)

Introduction

My pregnancies and births were straightforward and as easy as I expected pregnancies and births to be. I gave birth to my eldest twenty years ago in Tzefas, a small town in northern Israel. In the months before, some friends and I enjoyed the social outlet of an exercise class while gaining stamina and helping our babies in utero. For the births, we each took with us a companion who had been through birth before and could give us emotional as well as physical support. We had never heard of doulas, professional labor assistants, or coaches (all terms that essentially mean the same thing).

Although we all came from various religious backgrounds, none of us thought of the concept of birthing with a professional birth assistant by our side. But it is a concept as old as the Torah itself. Shifrah and Puah, better known as Yocheved and Miriam, were the original midwives, each with her unique role, about which Rashi speaks (*Shemos* 1:16). When people talk about this "new" concept of support for women in childbirth, I tell them how they've got it all backward.

While working as a professional labor assistant in Jerusalem, I began to realize that women looked upon birth as an event to endure. Their main question was "How can I get through this with as little pain as possible and as quickly as possible?" Instead of looking at this major life's transformation as a time of growth or a journey to be experienced and have memories to treasure, women were looking for ways to avoid or escape the experience entirely.

> Comfort in childbirth has been defined as a state of equilibrium and harmony. It's not the absence of pain because some degree of pain can be tolerated. To each woman and for each birth it can vary. Suffering, however, the spiritual component of pain, cannot coexist with comfort because it brings or is the result of disharmony.*

Birth should be a positive, challenging adventure. It is a time for physical and spiritual growth. It is a time to test ourselves to our limits and beyond at a time when we are transformed from having a mother to becoming a mother.

It is also a time to be thankful to Hashem for the merit to bring a Jewish soul into this world. There are many roles we fill on this search, but none are as rewarding as the role of birthing and raising a member of the Jewish people. With such an important task, we have to do our *hishtadlus*. As with any worthwhile venture, it becomes more meaningful when we put effort into it. When a mother-to-be learns about childbirth, exercises,

---

* S. L. M. Jimenéz, "Establishing a common vocabulary for exploring issues of pain and comfort," *The Journal of Perinatal Education* 5 no. 3 (1996): 53–57.

and eats nutritiously, she has a better chance of enjoying the pregnancy and having a safer outcome.

As I once heard at a doula conference in America, "Birth matters: how we birth matters." Yes, having a healthy mom and baby is the priority, but the process is important, too. Ask an eighty-five-year-old woman about her births of sixty years prior, and she will remember. Being treated with respect and dignity while being given emotional and physical support is critical for the birthing mom. It makes the difference between a lifetime of positive memories or the opposite.

I decided to compile and assist in the writing of stories that I hope will give strength, bolster courage, and even add some humor as women take this journey. As with any adventure, you may trip and fall or have some setbacks. Let's focus on the positive. If you are on bed rest, use the time wisely to write those overdue letters, learn something new, or pick up that needlepoint that's been collecting dust. If you have high blood pressure, use that as a signal to slow down, eat healthier, or reduce stress. Whatever test Hashem may present you with, learn from it, grow from it, and come closer to Him. You don't want to miss this opportunity of a lifetime.

Sarah Goldstein, CD (DONA)

Strength through Emunah

Rebbetzin Yitty Neustadt

This is a story about my grandmother during the Holocaust as I heard it from my father, Rav Ezriel Tauber. He is the oldest child and the only one to be born before the Holocaust. When he was a year old, the Nazis, *yemach shemam*, entered Czechoslovakia. The family was living in Pressburg at the time. Immediately after the Nazis occupied Czechoslovakia, my grandparents escaped to Hungary, and so they went from place to place, finding different ways to remain in hiding — sometimes as non-Jews, once as the family of a famous painter. Even in the midst of all this instability, my grandparents continued to build their family and to have children, just like in normal times.

Between 1940 and 1944, my grandmother had four sons. In 1944, one year before the end of the war, she was taken to Auschwitz. She was in her ninth month, pregnant with her fifth child. My father was six years old, and the youngest was a year and a half.

Once the *rav* called my grandfather and said to him, "You should know that your wife is the only woman in town (a very observant town) who goes to immerse! Please help me convince other families not to be afraid and to continue their lives as usual." (At the time, there were still high hopes in Hungary that the Germans wouldn't reach them. In any case, women were afraid, as in Egypt, to bear children.)

Grandfather spoke to many people to persuade them to keep having children, and they all said to him, "What? In times like this to continue building a family? It is madness when one doesn't know what will be tomorrow!"

My grandmother didn't make such calculations; she bore three sons during the war. She was pregnant with the fifth child when the Nazis found her and her family one Shabbos eve in their hiding place and captured all of them.

They were taken straight to Auschwitz, she to the special section for pregnant women. My grandmother understood immediately that this was the end. Suddenly Dr. Mengele, *yemach shemo v'zichro*, came in and said he wanted to conduct an experiment in hastening a birth. Who wanted to be the guinea pig? (As if they had a choice.) My grandmother understood that maybe all was lost anyway and agreed to be the first. He performed the experiment on her, and she had a healthy baby girl. He took the baby from her immediately, and she remained in bed in the "hospital."

Two hours after the birth she heard that this was her last stop before the gas chambers. She got out of bed and escaped from there, in the direction of the work camp. Due to divine providence, her sister-in-law found her.

Alarmed, she asked my grandmother, "Where did you come from? What happened to you?" My grandmother told her she had just given birth only two hours before.

They hid her under some rags and brought her a bit of bread and water, and she remained in hiding there for an entire year. She never even received a number or went out to work.

When the war was over, my grandfather told everyone, "I'm waiting for my wife to return." They laughed at him. What woman who had been taken to Auschwitz in her ninth month would come back alive? (How my grandfather and all the children stayed alive is a miracle in itself.)

My grandmother returned to him nine months later.

Slowly she regained her strength and health. Except for the baby girl, the entire family merited to immigrate to Eretz Yisrael after the Holocaust. She had another son and four daughters, and today she has much *nachas* from the entire family. Today one of her sons is a *rosh kollel,* and the others are *roshei yeshivah* and *maggidei shiur.*

My father asked her once, "How did you do it? Did you really think you would all survive?"

She answered, "Not at all! But we believe in the resurrection of the dead! When one bears a child, it is eternal! I never thought for a minute we were better than any of the millions who sanctified Hashem's Name with their deaths. I didn't think that our fate would be any different. But I did my task. We don't make calculations!"

She told me once that she was very careful and protected herself as much as possible in Auschwitz in order to stay alive. She told me, "I didn't think I would come out of there alive. But I didn't want to die because of some careless act on my part, because of not protecting myself enough. I made the maximum effort so that I would have the strength to continue — to live one more day, one more hour — in order to sanctify Hashem's Name in my death whenever they would come to take my life. I did not let myself succumb to the difficult conditions."

Today she has more than twenty great-great-grandchildren. Her adage is "Be happy that you are alive! Appreciate the gift of life, with faith and wholeheartedness."

Hashem runs the world measure for measure. She loved life and gave life and protected life, so she received her life back and the lives of her husband and sons.

Baby Building

Based on a true account heard by the author

S. N. Busch

As I awoke, violent shaking immediately overtook me. I doubled over in bed, totally overwhelmed by waves of nausea the likes of which I had never imagined possible. Sure, I had heard of morning sickness, suddenly turning green and running to the nearest restroom. I had heard of being exhausted, unable to do anything. But this absolute and total incapacitation had caught me by surprise.

Was it really just a few weeks ago that I was busy morning till night with my job, community projects, friends' and family's *simchah*s, and every Torah *shiur* I could cram into my schedule?

In the time that had passed since then, I hardly recognized myself. Even the thought of cooking a simple dinner for my husband and myself evoked waves of nausea. As often as not, such deep contemplation was followed by a dash down the hall. (Those dashes being among the few times I ventured out of bed during the day.)

The few who knew of my present state offered all sorts of potions and suggestions. "Eat before getting out of bed every morning," said one. "Ginger candy, ginger ale, try them — they helped my daughter," offered another. "Fresh air worked wonders for me. Turn on a fan by your head if you can't get out," from a third. "I just read an article that says nutritionists recommend potato chips to help with pregnancy-induced nausea," from yet another well-meaning relative.

Nutritionists recommending potato chips? I wondered. But then, the whole world seemed to have turned upside down. I hadn't informed many people of my current state of affairs. But they wondered at my sudden disappearance. When they did see me, some fretted, "You've lost weight," or, "You look pale. Are you feeling all right?" One particular neighbor, quite on the ball, but not wanting to invade my space, confided, "I always lose ten to fifteen pounds at the beginning of my pregnancies."

"So how are you spending your time now?" people would ask. What was I supposed to tell them?

Sometimes I would start feeling down, frustrated with my extreme incapacitation. Tears came so easily now, facilitated by my surging hormones. Who was I anyway? Was this the wife my husband had married? And, most importantly, would this ever end?

I tried to convince myself to be positive. Everything I was experiencing was a real *berachah*. This goes with the territory, with the curse of Chavah. It sometimes comes with being pregnant. At least my birth should be easy, the baby healthy. I decided to get my priorities right. Complaining wouldn't make the nausea any easier to endure. Brooding was getting me nowhere fast. Time for some old-fashioned distraction.

I decided to call Bina. Bina was half friend, half big sister, always a joy to talk to. She'd moved overseas a couple of years earlier. Our warm relationship had faded with the physical distance. But now that the international phone rates had plummeted... I began to dial.

Bina squealed with excitement, asking me what I was doing with my life. I deflected her question by asking her about her various activities. Bina loved to talk; she could have been a standup comedienne. I doubled over with laughter as tears ran down my cheeks. It was just the prescription I needed.

But then a powerful wave of nausea overtook me quite suddenly. I thanked Bina for the laughs and excused myself for the abrupt cutoff. I put down the phone and breathed slowly, Lamaze style. Within a few minutes, I managed to pass through the wave relatively unscathed.

My breathing returned to normal. Bina was an absolute angel. *At least I don't have to wait,* I reflected. *At least that. That would be far more painful than everything I'm going through now.* Bina, I knew, in all her enthusiasm about her work and "her girls," would have been thrilled to be in my place, to be wondering if she still had to *bentch* now that everything she had managed to get down had made its way back up in one burning swoop. To feel her clothes growing looser from lack of appetite. To feel overwhelmed by the new life growing inside her.

To know that I was building a baby, my very own baby, whom, I prayed, I would be holding in my arms in a few short months.

I put a hand on my stomach, trying to picture what was going on in there. The rapid growth into limbs and organs from a microscopic drop on its way to becoming a full-fledged person. Amazing how one cell multiplies to 6 billion. And I recalled that at the same time this body was physically being prepared for the outside world, its *neshamah* was being spiritually prepared as an angel taught it the entire Torah.

Amazing developments going on in there amidst the nausea and the fatigue, I mused. *It certainly is hard work.* I felt tired and lay back down.

I opened my eyes as I heard my husband walk in the door toward the end of the day. He put down his things and immediately peeked into the bedroom to check on me. "How are you?" he asked. "What have you been doing today?"

I smiled. "I have been building a baby."

> *Editor's note:* Most nausea and vomiting occur in the first trimester. In approximately 70 percent of pregnancies, although uncomfortable and distressing, it causes no harm to the baby who, in any case, gains the least weight in this trimester. There are a variety of tips in most pregnancy books that will help reduce the discomfort as well as alternative treatments, such as acupressure and homeopathic remedies. When the vomiting causes an excess of weight loss of 5 percent or more and is accompanied by dehydration, this usually can be eased through intravenous fluids. A doctor must be consulted.

They Will Turn

Gila Shoshanah Atwood

My first babies were twins. I call them my *"lechem mishneh"* because they were born on *erev Shabbos*, just like the double portion of manna, the *"lechem mishneh,"* was given on *erev Shabbos* during the forty years the Jewish people wandered in the desert.

I remember that I was so utterly new to the birth process I had no idea what to expect. I prayed and prayed for those babies to emerge finally. I wouldn't have minded hopping into a time machine to fast-forward to the time I could just look at their darling little faces.

I wasn't afraid of the birth. I had attended birth preparation classes with my husband, and I felt good about it, but I was impatient. Since they were twins, we expected them earlier than the due date. The official due date felt late!

I took a lot of walks so I would be nice and strong for the birth. Our apartment was perched on the top floor of a building in downtown Jerusalem, accessible by a twisting, soaring staircase, and this gave me the opportunity for a good cardiovascular workout.

My doctor was sure I was going to have a cesarean birth. An ultrasound in the eighth month revealed that the babies were not in cooperative positions. One was breech, the other transverse.

We consulted the Rebbe of Toldos Aharon. He said, "They'll turn." I must admit I wondered how that could possibly happen. However, despite my British skepticism, I decided not to worry and wait and see what would be. A month or so later another ultrasound showed that both babies were now heads up. Both breech. My husband went back to the Rebbe and asked if we should do a well-known *segulah* for making babies turn.

"No need. They'll turn," the Rebbe said confidently.

I waddled around like a penguin right until the end. Penguins became my theme. My husband went out and bought me pictures of penguins and penguin soft toys. I loved to walk, but the pregnancy slowed me down a lot, especially when I would get a painful mammoth stitch in my side. I had to rearrange the babies with gentle lateral shoves to literally get them off my nerves.

On Thursday evening, October 30, 1986, I was feeling stir-crazy and had to go for a walk. I strolled over to some friends who lived about fifteen minutes' waddle away, all the while strongly suspecting that "something" was finally happening, some small indefinable ache in the back every now and again.

My friend advised me to go to the hospital to get checked out. At the hospital I was told I was having contractions every four minutes.

"Oh, really?" I said in surprise.

The midwife also told me that the babies were moving around like the sons of Rivkah, performing synchronized swimming apparently.

This was the miracle! They had begun to turn all by themselves!

I slept little that night and did not make major progress by the morning. The young doctor who examined me suggested I go home. With twins! On *erev Shabbos*!

Believe it or not, we actually caught a bus and headed home. I davened on the bus, and when I reached the words "*shomei'a tefillah* — who hears our prayers," I felt a sensation that seemed definitely meaningful. It was a strong and painful contraction. *Wow!* I thought. *If this is the beginning, what will the rest of the birth be like?*

I signaled to my husband and told him what was happening. We thought, well, this could take ages. Let's go home and see how it goes. I walked from Davidka Square (in the center of town) to our tiny place on Malchei Yisrael Street, stopping every few minutes with more intensely meaningful sensations. Akiva suggested we buy challos for Shabbos. Somehow he also managed to buy a small blue stuffed penguin.

A mere two hours later — after a shower, a brief nap, a phone call, painfully staggering down the steps, and an exciting taxi ride up the main road — I was back at the hospital and fully ready to give birth.

A good friend told me to put the *sefer No'am Elimelech* by Reb Elimelech of Lizhensk under my pillow and to chant over and over, "*Shivisi Hashem l'negdi samid* — I put God before me always," both *segulah*s for an easy birth. It was an interesting exercise in timing to manage that and Lamaze breathing, but I did it, and before I knew it, I heard three unbelievable and totally surprising, joy-bringing words: "You can push!"

"I can push?" (What about that operation my doctor was so sure about? Apparently, my first baby was presented perfectly, head down! The turn, which began the previous evening, had been successful.)

"Yes! You can push!"

"I can push!"

"So push already!"

"Okay, great, wow. Will you please tell me when, because I can't feel the contractions anymore."

I was hooked to a fetal monitor, which told me when I was having a contraction; otherwise I couldn't know. I was numb. No painkiller, just numb. Transition, at the end of the labor, had been all back pain and pretty rough and then...nothing.

I listened to the monitor and soon realized I should push when the sounds grew faint. That proved as reliable as the nurse's prompting.

And then came Aharon! A boy! Could this mean a *pidyon haben*? It sure did!

He needed a little help coming out with forceps since he had a beautiful broad cranium. Perhaps he'd be very smart. I was already in awe of the little person.

And then, less than ten minutes later and with a little help from suction, my sweet daughter was delivered. They showed her to me right away. She already had feathery blonde hair, and it was love at first sight. This would be Sarah. Though not technically the firstborn, I think of her that way. She tells me she remembers vividly how her brother shoved her out of the way in order to be born first. Could this be? I have heard about people being put under hypnosis to reexperience their birth. Ah, well, already eager to be part of a mitzvah, that of *pidyon haben*.

After the births I just lay there blissfully, saying, "I don't believe it! I don't believe it! I don't believe it!"

Two beautiful human beings were actually born on

their official due date, each just under six and a half pounds and perfectly normal and healthy.

Two beautiful babies who had performed a double circus act in the span of just twelve hours. They had wriggled out of impossible positions that had me psyched for a cesarean and neatly positioned themselves in the standard, textbook, head-down position, and they didn't even get their cords tangled! My gratitude and sense of wonder was profound.

Over Forty-five

"Did you hear that I had a baby?" I questioned an acquaintance whom I saw at a wedding. Her face registered shock as she exclaimed, "No way!" Apparently she had not seen me in the last few months, when my growing middle notified people of the upcoming great event. I showed her my darling little baby, and it dawned on her that I was not pulling her leg; I had indeed had a baby. "*Mazel tov*," she proclaimed warmly and added her blessing that I merit to see much *nachas* from this little one, as well as my other children. I appreciated her good wishes and was not perturbed by her initial reaction of disbelief, since I am at the stage of life where one would sooner expect me to announce the birth of a grandchild than of a child.

About a month ago I delivered a healthy, beautiful baby boy. He is fought over by his adoring older siblings and has already brought much joy to our home. About a year ago, my youngest — a girl of close to six — declared, "I don't want to be the baby of the family. I want you to have another baby." I was close to forty-six at the time, although I have been told that I look younger, and I certainly feel younger.

I didn't think there was much chance of Bracha's wishes coming true, but I encouraged her to put in her request with the One above. "If Hashem wants, we will have another baby. Why don't you daven to Hashem, and we will see what happens?"

I guess I underestimated the power of the *tefillos* of a six-year-old. I was soon informed that my pregnancy test was positive, and Hashem did indeed want to bestow another blessing on our home.

I will admit that it took me a while to get used to the idea of having another child. Was I ready to drag through a pregnancy, deal with the sleepless nights, find the patience for a toddler? Would we have the energy to raise another child? I am a firm believer that you are only as old as you feel, so we would have to focus on feeling young and enthusiastic for a while. And there is something to be said for older parents. What we lack in youth we make up for in experience.

Perhaps I should start this story many years earlier, about twenty-five years ago. As a young couple, we assumed we would become young parents within a year or so. The months, then years, slipped by, with no news. We kept our spirits up by reminding each other that when the time would be right, Hashem would send us children. Thank God, after several years our family began to grow and grow. Each new arrival was greeted with gratitude and joy. The years we spent childless were long past, but they left an awareness that each additional child is a miracle and a gift. So when a well-meaning nurse asked me if I was happy about my latest pregnancy, I just looked at her. If Hashem decided to bestow another gift upon us, of course I was willing to accept.

On my first visit to the doctor I sought to clarify certain concerns. "What about my age?" I inquired.

"If you are healthy" (which, thank God, I am) "then there are no special considerations."

"What about the health of the baby?"

The doctor informed me that there was only a slightly higher risk for me than for a young mother, and I realized that my best policy was to pray that all would go well.

And it did. I was fortunate to have a relatively easy pregnancy and was able to keep up a full schedule, including exercise. I attribute it to prayer, mostly that of my mother. Praying for her loved ones is one of my mother's favorite hobbies. I am also fortunate to live in Israel, the land of miracles, and events like this are taken in stride. (When I had my seventh child in America, ten years earlier, I was treated like a freak — a "grand multipara of advanced age.")

The months passed quickly, and soon I found myself in my ninth month — still running around, with the assistance of support stockings and a daily short nap. In fact, three hours before delivery I walked down over a hundred steps to wish *mazel tov* at a *kiddush* and then walked up the stairs on the way back.

It was Shabbos and time to serve the *seudah*. I had begun to feel some contractions earlier in the morning, but ignored them since my past labors had progressed slowly. During the *seudah* I felt contractions about eight minutes apart and assumed things were on the way. After the meal was over, I washed the dishes and realized it was time to contemplate going to the hospital. For a variety of reasons, calling a Magen David Adom ambulance seemed the most appropriate choice. During the fifteen-minute ambulance ride, I felt a few strong contractions. When we arrived at the hospital, I was wheeled from the ambulance, but then allowed to walk into the examining room. My husband went to the desk to register.

"Go to the bathroom , and then I will examine you," instructed the midwife. Then she reconsidered and suggested, "On second thought, let me examine you first."

I situated myself on the examining table and allowed the midwife to examine me — and got ready to go through the most intensive part of labor, being hooked up to a monitor and perhaps to an IV as well. Imagine my surprise when the midwife proclaimed, "The baby is ready to come out. You can begin pushing." I pushed on the next contraction, and out came the baby. My husband arrived in the examining room one minute later and was greeted with the surprising news, "*Mazel tov*, it's a boy!"

The midwife kept repeating what a good thing it was that she had decided to examine me, and we all felt this easy birth was yet another facet of the gift.

Many people have wished us well, and I feel they truly share in our *simchah*. "I was so excited to hear about your baby." "I am so happy for you. May you have much *nachas* from him." "Your children are so fortunate. And the baby is so lucky to be born into a family with so many older siblings." "I called America to spread the news." "This is amazing. Hashem should give you strength." "May you raise him to Torah, *chuppah*, and good deeds and dance at his wedding."

I was fortunate to have a quick recovery and am enjoying every minute of attending to the baby — even in the middle of the night. Of course, I have to share the baby with his siblings, but they graciously allow me to feed him and take midnight duty.

We named the baby Yehudah to express our gratitude for our gift at this point in our lives and to thank Hashem for having the confidence in us that we are young enough to have the energy to raise this bundle of joy.

> This story was written by a well-known author and *rebbetzin*. If anyone wishes to contact her, she may do so through the editor, Sarah Goldstein, at emgee@netvision.net.il.

Birth Surprise in Jerusalem

Batya Solomon

Our twins remained in the breech position for months before their due date. We were unable to find a midwife or doctor willing to let me birth naturally unless at least the first baby turned head down. I had already tried doing special exercises, which didn't work, and no medical people would risk attempting to turn them externally.

Our other children were born at home, but that possibility seemed quite remote, given our babies' positions. I had already reached the thirty-eighth week with both twins still head up under my rib cage.

I was eating enormous amounts of protein and calcium, resting, and waiting for the big event. Neighborhood girls were taking turns helping out with our kids, and my husband was doing overtime, acting as both mom and dad, while I rested on the couch.

When I went for a checkup, our local family doctor was surprised that I still had not contacted a surgeon.

"Don't you want to know who will hold the knife?" he asked bluntly. Reluctantly I realized he was right. I searched for an obstetrician with expertise in twin deliveries. He agreed to let me have a "trial of labor" to see if they would turn before doing an operation.

Baruch and I decided to visit Ma'ayan Sataf, a much-acclaimed special spring located on the outskirts of Jerusalem. I had heard that this was known to help turn breech babies and ensure an easy birth. Our last chance! When we sought advice of three tzaddikim regarding this *segulah*, one told us to drink the waters in a specially prescribed order. A different tzaddik said to say a certain *perek* of *Tehillim* while looking at the spring, and the third rabbi said to follow both suggestions. We also had the assurance of a blessing from an especially beloved rabbi whom we always spoke with before each of our children's births.

Many people were praying for us. I had asked all who knew our situation to keep us in mind. But I was still exceedingly anxious that all should work out well.

When we reached the ancient site, my husband and I first drank from the spring, then sat beside a tree, recited psalms, and davened, feeling both the sanctity of the place and the intensity of our request: "Please let them be born without complications, healthy and whole! Please, God, let the babies turn!"

It was a strenuous climb back up to the parking lot, not an easy feat for a woman in late pregnancy who had barely walked to the corner store for the last two months. We reached the car and drove back home, anxious but hopeful that we had done our *hishtadlus*. Like everything, the way they would be born was up to God.

I did not want a cesarean birth, especially since I had had major abdominal surgery and numerous small operations over the last twenty years. I also wanted to avoid the risk of infection and having to recover from surgery while taking care of newborn twins along with our other young children. I knew, however, that I would have to accept the fact that the risk of complications was too great to take any chances delivering naturally.

I had not had any Braxton-Hicks contractions that entire week, which is quite unusual for me in my ninth month, and especially considering I was carrying twins. I had already been hospitalized during the thirty-fourth week because of contractions that would not stop. Fortunately an IV had hydrated me, and the pregnancy had continued normally. Now, four weeks later, I felt like I would be pregnant forever.

We made it home safely from the spring, but I didn't feel the babies turn. That Friday night, after our meal, when all the kids were asleep, I took a walk with our guest, Miriam. My friend Sara Rifka had suggested she come for Shabbos. "Just in case Batya needs you," she had told Miriam.

When I returned home, it was already after midnight, and the summer heat made it impossible to sleep. Restless, I read all night, finally dozing off at around 5 a.m. At about six thirty I was suddenly awakened by a very intense contraction, the kind I usually feel at the end of my typically ten-hour labors. I got out of bed and stood, wavering, and immediately felt the need to use the bathroom. Then I realized what I really felt was a baby ready to be born!

I panicked — two breech babies! No time to think. I rushed back to the bedroom and told my husband, who was instantly awake, that I felt I needed to push. He remained calm and collected, which was a good thing because I certainly did not.

I had had no labor, no warning. I couldn't fight the urge to push, so I quickly put a towel on the bed, lay down on my side, and simply let my body work. My waters broke, and Baruch quickly called an ambulance. He explained that I was not having any contractions, but my waters had broken, and there were two babies who were breech. Then we called the obstetrician who was supposed to do the cesarean.

"I won't make it to Ein Kerem Hospital," I yelled into the phone.

"Don't worry, I will make sure a top physician will meet you at the closest hospital," he answered calmly.

As soon as we hung up the phone, Baruch asked me if I could get off the bed and stand, which we had read was the most favorable position for a breech birth.

"No!" I shouted, but after only a moment of hesitation, almost by instinct, I managed to get off the bed as quickly as possible, grabbed the top of the radiator for support, and our first baby was born! A frank breech!

"It's a boy!" Baruch announced. He gently moved him out of the way. Thank God, our baby was red (which meant he was getting enough oxygen) and crying. Then our daughter emerged, miraculously turned head first and wailing, within three minutes of her big brother.

Everything had happened so fast. Ten long minutes after we had called the ambulance the driver arrived, burst into the room, and was greeted by our relieved, amazed announcement, "Everything's okay now!"

"What? Why didn't you call me?" the ambulance driver shouted, his eyes wide with shock.

"We did! Right away!" we answered.

Within moments all of our children, who had thankfully slept through the excitement, were wide awake and running in to greet the new arrivals to our family. The ambulance driver, highly agitated by our calmness, insisted on whisking us away to the hospital to check the babies and me and make sure everything really was okay. Thank God, Miriam was there to watch everyone.

I was carried out to the ambulance, with Baruch and another paramedic holding the twins. Smiling broadly, I glanced up at our building and noticed our neighbor's children staring openmouthed from their window. They certainly were shocked to see me transported to the waiting vehicle with two babies in tow!

The news about our babies' arrival traveled faster by word of mouth than e-mail. That an unassisted birth with such a high potential for life-threatening complications had gone so smoothly was considered nothing short of an astounding miracle.

Everyone who heard was shocked that my bearded, "ultra-Orthodox" rabbinic husband was the only one there to help me. "So tell us how you learned your midwifery technique?" he was questioned half-jokingly. But Baruch and I knew that the real midwife was God alone.

My Cesarean Birth Experience

*Or, If you Have to Have One,
Do It This Way*

Ruthy Alexander

"A spot of trouble" is what the doctor said. Having had six regular births, it came as a shock to hear these words. My husband and I visited the head of the department to discuss a few details of the previous birth experience and to get me a thorough checkup. The previous birth ended with burst veins, which required extensive suturing while I was under general anesthesia. Since there was a high chance that this would happen again, especially at the pushing stage, the doctor recommended that a cesarean birth be scheduled.

I had many preconceived ideas about this type of operation, many fears and reservations. So with only a few weeks until my due date, I started to do some serious research. My good friend Malka had undergone several births by cesarean with a special technique that she assured me would enable a speedy recovery. We quickly made an appointment to see the gynecologist and to book a date for the operation.

All this was happening during the sweltering summer — my due date was a week before Tishah B'Av. I happened to know, from an ultrasound, that it was highly likely to be a boy. That meant a *shalom zachor*, bris, and bar mitzvah during the Nine Days. I didn't want to tell my husband it was probably a boy since it could have raised his excitement level and his blood pressure! And so, when the doctor scheduled me for the operation during the Nine Days, in the thirty-eighth week, I asked if we could schedule it a few days earlier since the baby was already large enough.

My lovely baby boy was born before the Nine Days, weighing in at 4 kilograms (9 pounds). I can't imagine what his weight would have been if he had gone to term!

If I had to have a cesarean, better to think about the advantages:

1. a shorter pregnancy in the middle of a hot summer;
2. a good night's sleep before the due date so I had plenty of energy for the big day;
3. no waking up neighbors in the middle of the night, as we did with the other five births;
4. being able to walk better than after the previous births and to dance with joy with my lovely son (probably due to my veins having been so painful); and

5. hiring a private caregiver, which I normally would not have given myself the luxury to do.

So, even though I missed out on the various benefits of a regular birth, and a cesarean can be more risky, if I had to have one, I'm glad I made the most of it!

Taxi Baby

Esther Shurin

I was a week overdue. This is the stage where you just sit around and wait for the baby to make its appearance. We were pretty nervous by then and busy making sure all the arrangements were in place — the babysitter, the suitcase, and so forth. The usual questions were raised: What if it's on Shabbos? What if someone is sick? What if it never happens? (It sometimes feels like that, but my sister assured me that there have been no recorded cases of permanent pregnancy!)

One night we were listening to the radio, and we heard a story about a baby who was born in a taxi in Haifa. The cord was wound around his neck three times. The taxi driver took off the cord and saved the baby's life. I looked at my husband and he looked at me. He was absolutely horrified. After a brief silence, he asked me, "How did the taxi driver know what to do?"

"Don't be silly," I said. "I'm not having any baby in a taxi! What are you worried about?"

Famous last words.

One cold winter night I finally started having contractions, but they weren't too serious. I didn't feel well, and my stomach was upset, which slowed me down considerably. I figured things were finally happening, and I had better get ready. I got dressed, got my stuff together, woke my husband up, and prepared to leave. All of this took time since I really felt terrible. Finally we called a cab, and he went upstairs to get the babysitter while I started walking up the two flights of stairs to the parking lot to wait for the cab.

It was about four thirty in the morning, cold and absolutely still. The contractions were getting stronger and longer, and my teeth were chattering from cold and nerves. Where was the cab? Where was my husband?

All of a sudden, with tremendous force, my waters broke. I felt the baby's head engage, and panic set in. I had no idea what to do, and I don't think I've ever been so terrified in my life. Crazy thoughts chased each other in my head. Should I go home? (Can't do the stairs.) Should I give birth in the parking lot? (Not an attractive thought.) Help!

Just then the taxi pulled up, and my husband came with the suitcase (*baruch Hashem*). "Sit in the front!" I told him. There was no way I could sit with the baby coming, so I threw myself into the back seat. The pain and the fierce contractions were impossible to slow down. I did not want to have this baby in the taxi, but I knew I didn't have time. How could I stop this birth from happening?

As the intensity of the contractions built up, I realized I did not want to stop this birth either; it was too powerful. I wasn't exactly quiet about all this, and I could see the taxi driver's white face in the mirror.

"Shaare Zedek," my husband told him.

"Are you crazy?" he yelled. "We're going to the nearest hospital!"

At that time of night, it's about a ten-minute drive from our apartment to Har HaTzofim Hospital. Shaare Zedek is about twenty minutes. The driver drove like mad, but even at that speed he couldn't shorten the drive enough to prevent the inevitable.

I was crying from the overwhelming pangs. It was an incredibly quick birth. After two minutes I was screaming, "There's the head! There's the baby!" but they didn't need me to announce it because by then we could hear, *baruch Hashem*, the cries of the newborn filling the car.

The tremendous relief of hearing that baby cry is indescribable, after the terror of that birth in the car and the fears of what if something went wrong, God forbid! Thank God, nightmares of the cord around the neck receded, and I began to relax. After all, as far as I was concerned, the worst was over.

"Is it a boy or a girl?" I asked, understandably curious since I had three little girls at home. My husband had turned around and grabbed the baby to keep it from falling off the seat. We had nothing to cover it with, and we were only minutes from the hospital. To me the question of boy or girl was very reasonable. When you give birth in the hospital, they tell you right away. In my preternaturally calm state, it seemed odd to me that my husband was so frazzled, but he thought my question was crazy. "It's dark in here. I can't see anything! Are you out of your mind?"

Undeterred, I reached over to feel the baby. "It's a boy!" I shouted.

Filled with delight and excitement, I noticed that the two men did not share my elation. I figured that now that I felt better it was their turn to panic. I was just so happy it was all over. The baby was crying, and it was a boy! In the meantime, the poor driver radioed ahead for a midwife to be ready. My husband was beyond words; he was a complete wreck. By then I was able to focus a bit, and I spent the rest of that memorable ride apologizing to the driver for doing this to him. He was really nice about it. "This is natural, lady. It happens," he said, but it was quite clear to me that he was not too happy to have this particular "natural" experience.

The midwife wasn't there when we pulled up. Someone opened the car door, saw the baby there, and slammed it shut again. It was March, after all, and very cold. The rest was pure comedy. Everyone was screaming, "Where's the midwife? Where's the midwife?" and running back and forth. She finally came, cut the cord, and carried my son off. I was put on a stretcher and rolled in.

For two days I did not sleep a wink. It was actually Friday morning, and I spent a very quiet Friday and Shabbos in the hospital, but I kept replaying that crazy scene in my mind. I could not believe I had actually had the baby in a taxi. *Other* people do things like that, not *me*!

My parents taped the conversation when my husband called them with the news. Then they called my brothers and sisters and taped that, too, so I got to hear my mother saying, "Don't tell anyone. It's such a crazy thing to do!" My father didn't think it was so crazy. "No, it isn't. It's natural. It happens all the time!" And I got to hear my husband complaining, "It took two minutes, but it seemed like *hours!*"

It was pretty funny that my mother wanted to keep it a secret, since it was on the radio and most of Yerushalayim heard about it one way or another. My husband's students were all agog to hear how he had delivered the baby. That was really a laugh. *No one delivered that baby; he did it all by himself!*

My husband had offered the driver money for any damage to the back seat of the car. They checked it out at the time, and it didn't seem too bad, but we gave him our number.

The taxi driver never asked us for the money. He did call and ask why we hadn't invited him to the bris. I guess I was too embarrassed. So silly of me, I really should have invited him... In a burst of guilt I sent him a huge *mishlo'ach manos* that Purim, a bottle of schnapps, and a photo of the baby. We never heard from him again. (Years later, perhaps feeling guilty that I did not call him for the bris, I invited him to the bar mitzvah. This took a good bit of detective work on my part. A name like Yossi Cohen in Yerushalayim is like John Smith in New York, and he had moved. He was really delighted to hear from us, but he didn't come.)

The strange part about this story is that when my son was two years old, my husband took a ride home in a taxi. He always shmoozes with the drivers, and he was discussing with this driver how our neighborhood had grown and the demand for taxis had increased. As they pulled up in front of our building, the driver casually mentioned to him, "Someone in your building had a baby in my taxi about two years ago." My husband was shocked. Then the driver said, "I never got paid for changing the seat cover."

Incurably honest, my husband spoke up. "That must have been my wife! But you aren't the driver who took us that night."

"Well," the driver continued, "I lent my taxi to a friend on Thursday night and guess what happened!

This woman gave birth in my car, and when I got it back Friday afternoon, it was a little the worse for wear!"

Somehow the owner had never gotten our information. As soon as my husband heard this, he pulled out some cash. "How much do you want?" and paid the owner of the taxi what he asked for.

I was a little annoyed. After all, two years had passed, and we had offered to pay. My husband looked at it differently. He said, "That man is walking around for two years with a grudge against our son. Don't you think Hashem keeps accounts? I'm glad he found me. It's terrible to think that he was upset at us for so long." Go argue with that.

That same week a former student of my husband's came by to apologize. He had owed us money for several years and had finally gotten around to paying. It was the exact amount of money that we had just paid the owner of the taxi! All my husband said was "You see, Hashem keeps accounts."

Day by Day
Shaindy in Monsey

Again? I'm almost forty. Eight kids are enough, I'd thought at thirty-seven. It's not the raising them, I mind. Eight wonderful, smart, active (*bli ayin hara*) kids. If not for the miscarriages it would have been more. It was the births.

Now, as I begin my ninth month, I remember having said (after the last birth), "I don't want to go through this again." Memory has a way of being selective, especially when it comes to a spectacular accomplishment that takes some challenge and invested effort. I remember that it was hard. I remember that it hurt. I don't remember the actual pain.

As the pregnancy progresses, I focus on the new life growing inside me. I want this birth to be different. It will be different. I will work to make it different. But how?

I read inspiring books on birth. I hire a labor coach. I learn HypnoBirthing, despite my doubts. I make a tape for myself of birth affirmations using relaxation music for the background.

Day by day I prepare.
Day by day I breathe.
Day by day I relax...let go...pray.

Then we get closer. My mom comes for a visit but has to leave by Monday. She lives two thousand miles away.

The doctor told me two weeks ago that the head was low. The contractions come and go for two weeks — every night, sometimes during the day, for hours. They come. They go.

I don't want to wait. The waiting is too long, the contractions too strong.

Castor oil? Okay. I'll try it. More contractions, more cramping...no baby.

I'm rushing...feeling pressured...more castor oil...no baby.

My doula says, "Wait. When he is ready, he will come."

They do come. When they are ready — not when we are ready.

Sunday night my contractions begin again. My mom is leaving tomorrow.

I breathe, I relax, I stay positive, I pray...

It's 5 a.m. My doula comes. Can I really do this again? I'm getting closer...soon a baby...

To the hospital. My mom comes with us. I can do this again. I try to stay focused.

I relax...I breathe...I know I am almost there...soon a baby...

I dilate quickly to eight centimeters. The doctor requests to break my waters. Fine with me. It used to go quickly after that. I remember and I know I can do this again...

Day by Day

He's born! He's beautiful! He latches on. I'm in love all over again.
I did do it again...my baby.

> *Editor's note*: Using castor oil, as well as other "natural" ways to bring on labor, will work only if the baby is ready to be born. Otherwise, it is best to use these means when your caregiver suggests induction (for a medical reason). It is desirable to consult your *rav* and seek a second medical opinion.

Wheelchair Birth

Sima Spetner

I was in my thirty-eighth week, pregnant with number 8. I am a bit overweight, and the additional weight of the pregnancy pushed my blood pressure up, and they decided to induce labor. I was not prepared for this. The new school year would be starting in exactly one week. My blood pressure had always been a little high. Did it have to shoot up now, with September 1 only one week away? There were still books to buy, skirts to hem, and shoes to get. The children were supposed to be well into a schedule when this baby was born.

On Tuesday evening they were going to give me pitocin to get the labor going, but the baby was still high and apparently not quite ready. They decided to postpone the induction. Instead I was to have hospital "bed rest" (isn't that a contradiction in terms?).

"For how long?" I asked.

"Until *motza'ei Shabbos*, and then we will see" was the reply.

I was put on blood pressure medication, which

helped the first day, but then it started to rise again. By *motza'ei Shabbos* they saw it was very high and told me I should undergo some tests, including an ultrasound.

Finding the ultrasound room was no easy task. I was in a major Jerusalem hospital, and the room was located at the far end. I would have to make my way down long passageways with the lights dimmed at that late hour. It was quite unnerving, but I had to go.

I decided not to call my husband since he had his hands full as it was, taking care of the kids. An ultrasound is a fairly simple procedure. If they decided to do anything else, I would call him to come.

Throughout the days I had to be in the hospital, I kept repeating in my mind, *I will be home on Tuesday when school starts. My kids are not going to start their first day of school without me!* Everyone thought I was crazy. I would have to give birth by the next morning, Sunday, to be out by Tuesday, and I was far from giving birth.

Finally I arrived at the ultrasound room, only to find it locked. I was distracted by the sound of someone crying and spotted a woman sitting in a wheelchair, apparently waiting for the ultrasound technician to arrive. She was there because her labor was not progressing. They suspected that the umbilical cord was wrapped around the baby's body, keeping it from coming out. They had sent her for an ultrasound to see if this was the cause. Whoever had wheeled her there had left her to take care of something (hopefully to find the technician). The woman had thrombosis so she was sitting with her leg bandaged. It would be impossible for her, in that condition and at her weight (almost twice my size), to wheel herself to find help.

As her contractions strengthened and became closer, I realized there was only one thing to do. "Let's go," I said courageously. I pushed her down those long corridors, trying to remember the way back to the delivery rooms, forgetting about my high blood pressure problem. Suddenly I felt contractions; I was in labor!

Her contractions were coming so fast that I was concentrating on finding my way back as quickly as possible. When we arrived, huffing, at the delivery rooms, the sight must have been amazing — me, in my ninth month, pushing my companion, almost double my size, and screaming, "She's about to give birth!" The midwives tilted the chair backward, put on their gloves, and, with me still holding the wheelchair, my new friend gave birth.

Thanks to her, and the exertion of pushing the wheelchair to the other end of the hospital, I gave birth forty-five minutes later!

She was always grateful to me, and we've been close for over ten years.

If that isn't a nice enough ending, my newfound friend has become *shomer Shabbos*.

When the Unexpected Occurs...

Naomi Grossman

I started labor on the night of 21 Sivan 5761 (June 11, 2001) after an ordinary day of doing as much housework as I was able at the end of a pregnancy. After I had put my five children to bed, I flopped down on the sofa, feeling very tired, and I started to feel the first contractions. To be precise, they were not really contractions, but strong and searing pains that were different from anything I had felt during my previous labors. As most of my children have either been born head facing my back (posterior position) or have turned only during labor, my early contractions usually take the form of back pains, and when these cut in and out regularly I know it is time to go to the hospital. This time it was different. I was not only experiencing backaches, but the most terrible abdominal pains. At first I did not even realize that these were labor pains until I noticed that they were cutting in and out.

I told my husband who, being used to the false labors that I generally go through before every birth, advised me to lie down and wait. It did not take us long to realize that it was not a good idea to wait for too long because these pains were becoming more and more intense.

"Let's get out of here," I suggested. "I'd rather be sent home again than take too much of a risk."

We got into the car and set off for the hospital, leaving my mother, who had come from abroad especially for the birth, in charge of the house.

It had been a fairly normal pregnancy, except that I looked much bigger than usual and I felt a lot more tired. My veins, which have always been a problem, had also been especially bad. My mother and I joked about how huge I looked, but the doctor had weighed me and found me no heavier than in my previous pregnancy. He suggested that maybe the baby would be slightly bigger than usual. My mother and I reckoned that since this was my sixth pregnancy in seven years, it was probably quite normal to look so big.

Now, as I set off for the hospital, I was looking forward to ending this long, arduous pregnancy. But I felt uneasy; the pain seemed so much worse than in my previous labors. By the time I got out of the car, I could hardly walk, and I was almost doubled over with each contraction. Yet somehow I made it into the hospital, where I was told that I was already fully dilated and that as soon as my waters broke I could give birth.

Although I have never taken pain relief of any sort during labor, this time I was in so much agony that I asked about an epidural. I was told it was too late. I consoled myself with the thought that if I had gone this far already without any pain relief, I would not have to be in pain for too much longer and that soon it would all be over!

By this time, I had very sharp pains in my back as well as strong contractions. To prevent the very real possibility of another posterior delivery or a face presentation, I was told to lie on all fours. In the past, I had delivered two of my babies face first, which I am told is extremely unusual. This is because, as posterior babies, they had tried to turn during delivery but got stuck on the way out. Face presentations can result in a cesarean delivery, but so far I have been fortunate enough to deliver naturally. However, delivering a face presentation baby is very painful, and I would have done absolutely anything to prevent it.

After around twenty minutes of lying on all fours, the midwife told me that she thought it would be best to break my waters because this was the only thing that was holding up delivery and there was no point in tiring myself out. By this time, I was in so much pain that I would have agreed to anything, and I nodded gratefully.

Within a few minutes, my son was born. As he crowned, the midwife called out, "I don't believe it!" She later told me that she watched his head descending in posterior position and how he made a 180-degree turn at the very last second, just before he came into the world, averting all possibility of a face presentation! In the end, his birth was so easy, and I felt such a sense of relief.

Yet that was not the only miracle that night. The best was yet to come. As I lay peacefully watching the nurses taking away my son to clean him up, I felt some more contractions starting up. I was so relieved that I had avoided the horrors of a face presentation and that this tiring pregnancy was now over. I felt more than ready to deliver the afterbirth.

Suddenly the midwife asked, "Did you do an ultrasound during your pregnancy?"

"No. Our custom is that we don't do them unless there's something wrong, and there wasn't." My contented, peaceful mood evaporated almost straightaway. *They don't usually ask questions like that unless there's a problem*, I thought, and I started to tense up.

"Why?" I asked suspiciously.

"Because we think you've got another baby in there," replied the midwife with a smile.

"That's not possible!" I blurted out. "There are no twins in either of our families, and I haven't taken any fertility drugs either."

"Let's take an ultrasound now, and we'll find out," continued the midwife.

The staff rolled a portable ultrasound monitor into the room, and within seconds the picture of another baby appeared on the screen.

"Oh yes," said the midwife with great satisfaction. "You've got another baby in there all right, head down and ready to go. As soon as you feel another contraction, push!"

Before I had even a moment to digest the fact that I was about to have another baby, I gave birth to a little girl. It was the easiest delivery I ever had. It was also the most shocking labor I had ever experienced. Usually it takes nine months to bring another baby into the world. In the case of my youngest daughter, it took just six minutes!

I will never forget the whirl of emotions that followed. Birth is always an emotional experience, even when it goes the way you expect it. However, the feeling that a mother has on the birth of another, unexpected baby is almost beyond description.

Moments later, I lay cradling the two babies, who had been placed on either side of me, looking back and forth between them. Neither my husband nor I could believe what had just happened. As my husband called my anxious mother with the incredible news that, not one, but two new grandchildren had been born, I felt a mixture of emotions. On the one hand, I was absolutely delighted. Both babies, neither of whom resembled the other, were absolutely adorable. On the other hand, I had no idea how I was going to cope. Managing one newborn baby is very taxing at the beginning. What was I going to do with two? And what about nursing? Did we have enough baby clothes? And what about everyday issues, like going out with twins plus a toddler who did not walk yet? And how would I manage with all my other children? And...and...and...

Now, looking back on these events at a distance of almost two years, I can really appreciate how much of a miracle the birth of my twins was. First of all, even without an ultrasound, it is still a riddle as to why my multiple pregnancy went undiagnosed. Later my doctor said he found it a most unusual case because it did not have any of the features of a twin pregnancy. For instance, one of the most basic signs is the sudden change in the shape of the uterus, yet in my case it did not change so drastically. Even more unusually, my weight gain during this pregnancy exactly mirrored the weight gained during the previous one — we even compared my charts week by week and the weights were the same, pound for pound.

I believe that for whatever reason Hashem did not want me to know that I was expecting twins until they were born. Maybe it was to spare me the worry many women go through during multiple pregnancies, as well as the possibility of the extra, unwanted medical attention that I probably would have received.

The other thing is the risk that was involved. Subsequently I read that in England the mortality rate among second twins that are born naturally is as high as 40 percent. The fact that my second twin was born so easily, with her head down and the right way around, is a miracle in itself. Both of the babies were also normal weights — at birth the boy was 2.8 kilograms (6.16 pounds), and the girl was 2.4 kilos (5.28 pounds). Whenever I hear about the problems many other mothers face following the birth of twins, such as a low birth weight or prematurity, I thank Hashem for making things work out the way they did.

Although most people were thrilled when they heard our story, I also heard pitying remarks such as "Oh, dear, twins after five such young children! Rather you than me!" My response to such sentiments is that if you are going to have a pregnancy that ends differently from how you expected, let it be only because you have delivered another healthy baby. Such surprises are a blessing, and they should only be welcomed.

Don't Overorganize

Sara Chana Yisrael

I had it all arranged two weeks before. I had written up a list of which child would be picked up by which person and delivered to which friend. I had tagged the bags of clothes for each one with their destinations and drivers written on the front. With five children, each going to a different family, this seemed like a major military maneuver.

I was sleeping soundly, when I woke and realized that my waters were breaking. I jumped up and grabbed a maxi diaper and got to a phone. I called a friend. She took a taxi right over, ready to have him waiting while I hobbled down four flights of steps. It seemed to take hours.

Friend B, my neighbor who was coming with me, was called over. She thought the cab wasn't going fast enough, so she suggested I make a few choice groans. That did the trick. We arrived in time to enjoy a peaceful half-hour of laboring followed by the birth of a gentle girl with very long fingers. At least one of my kids will be able to play the piano.

Later, my dear friend Zissy came to the hospital to visit, and she asked if I had heard what happened. I had no idea what she was talking about. She explained that everything that I had planned had gone in another direction. Each child ended up in the wrong person's house, driven by the wrong person, with the wrong bag of clothes.

I didn't care. I was enjoying a quiet stay at the hospital on the last days of Pesach with my new sweet little girl.

There's No Place Like Home

Lena Shore

"So," asked the woman in the flowered robe as she smeared cream cheese on her lightly toasted bread, "where did you give birth?"

"At home."

Silence.

"Excuse me?" asked another. "Was that on purpose?"

"Oh yes," I replied happily, continuing to stir the lumps out of my oatmeal.

"Wow." The woman in the flowered robe stopped eating. "I would love to do that. It sounds so wonderful and comfortable. Weren't you scared?"

"Well" — I tentatively tasted my oatmeal and added more milk from the pitcher on the table — "I had a midwife, and she brought everything with her."

"Oh." The woman with the heavy glasses shook her head in amazement. "Sounds fantastic. But what if you wanted an epidural?"

I paused for a moment, spoon in hand, then I answered firmly, "You would need to go to the hospital."

The woman nodded slowly, and conversation revolved around the value of epidurals. Afterward, and for the entire time I spent at the convalescent home for new mothers, I had the reputation of being somewhat of an expert on birth, especially natural birth. My home birth had made me a celebrity, but it was for far different reasons that I had chosen this way to bring my new baby into the world.

Misgav Ladach, a maternity hospital that espoused natural births, was no more, and with its closing the only place where I had felt comfortable giving birth became a memory. The void left behind caused many women to feel stranded with no place to have their babies. An overflow of women now surged into other hospitals, leading to overcrowding and factory-style births. I wanted something else. And I wanted my midwife, the one who had been there with me for the three previous births, to be with me again to give me a sense of security and safety. Hospitals had a policy that one could not use a private midwife, and so, with her usual enthusiastic style, she had bounced out of the hospital and into the world of home birthing.

She was very positive about a home-birth experience for me. Home births have been proven safe in low-risk births, and hospitals are wonderful for problems. Birth is generally not a problem. I live within half an hour from a major medical center, a critical criterion when it comes to home births. So I put together a team of four very special women around me to support and guide me through the birth journey.

But I still had to convince my husband. Naturally skeptical, he shares my visions in a logical and methodical manner. Scientific articles proving the low risk of home births, time spent explaining my feelings and concerns, and finally a feeling that he supported me (though I cannot say he has become a home-birth advocate) allowed me to proceed with my plans. I bought my supplies, prayed, and waited.

My midwife would arrive for the birth of my baby equipped with three large bags and an oxygen tank. In the end very little of the equipment was used. But it gave me great comfort to see the meticulous care that had gone into ensuring both mine and my baby's safety.

The night my baby was born was drizzly and cool. My husband was recovering from a nasty bout of bronchitis and had stayed home that day. I had been having contractions for days. They had kept misleading me into thinking that things were about to happen, and then they would disappointingly stop. I began to wonder how I would tell the difference between this false labor and the real thing.

The first clue I had was that I lost my appetite. This was most unusual since a special meal for Rosh Chodesh Adar had been prepared. My husband looked at me and then told the kids it was time to leave to go to our friends' home and maybe in the morning they would have a new baby brother or sister. They left with not a word of protest.

We contacted my team and let them know it was time. A special friend of mine was there before anyone else arrived. She put pressure on my lower back to relieve the pain of the contractions and helped me breathe through them.

Like my other labors, this one was promising to be mostly in my back, another posterior baby. As the night continued, I would sway, standing supported through each contraction with a caring hand pressed firmly on my back. Sitting through a contraction was not a possibility. My mind would wander between contractions, but as I felt the building of a new one, I would stand and rock and focus on getting through just this one, like I had learned so many years before. One contraction at a time.

My waters broke by the white bookshelf in our living room, and then I knew that a bath was out of the question. I stood under the shower, and the constant spray of warm water both soothed and focused me.

I was sure I must be making progress, so imagine my disappointment to discover that I had dilated slightly more than one centimeter in the course of four hours. My midwife didn't want to tell me at first, but I could tell by looking at her face that she had also expected more. Through the course of those first hours, she had monitored me while I was standing and kept asking me if I felt the baby moving. She had stayed back and let me work without rushing to check me. She actually took a nap on our couch to be ready for the real action.

A tinge of fear entered my heart. What if I couldn't make it? The contractions were intensifying, and it was getting more and more difficult to stay on top of each one. I felt my resolve and my energy waning. Thoughts of hospitals and drugs suddenly became very attractive. *This is why women take epidurals*, I thought.

"Would you like a cocktail?" my midwife asked me. This special concoction of herbs was made to take the edge off of each contraction and calm me. All through the labor she had been giving me homeopathic remedies to keep my labor moving forward. My first labor had stalled, and I had been put on pitocin to restart the contractions. My fear of this happening again colored all my labors. At the beginning of my labor, when I suddenly began to shake uncontrollably, my midwife had massaged me with oils. I had been calmed; the shaking had stopped. What could she do for me now?

"Go back into the shower," she said. I returned to the water stream, and the contractions began to climb one on top of the other, and I thought, *If she checks me again and I'm only six centimeters, I'm leaving. I'm catching the next bus and going home. Oh, yeah, I am home. No matter. I'm still leaving.*

These thoughts gave me some feeling of solace, and then I remembered in the less than thirty seconds that now came between contractions that these thoughts generally accompanied transition and that could mean I was reaching the end. My faithful supporter kept her hands on my back. Small yet filled with great strength she kept reminding me that each contraction was bringing me closer to meeting my baby.

Hello, baby, I thought, and then the contractions came one after another, a tidal wave in which I could only squat and bend into them.

"I feel pressure," I whispered hoarsely.

A half-hour after stepping into the shower, I emerged barely able to walk back to my bed to be checked and was cheerfully told, "You're all ready."

I had dilated six centimeters in under half an hour. My baby was ready to be born. With the support of the women in my team, I was lifted against the pillows on my bed and told to push with the next contraction.

I breathed in and tried to visualize the energy going down and out, down and out. At one point, things got a little scary. The cord was wrapped around the baby's neck. I had to push quickly because he was turning blue. Standing outside was my husband, who heard these words. He had remained outside the circle of women and gave his support from a distance. I knew he was there.

With a couple of final screams that came from deep within me, the baby was propelled out into the world. In an instant, the room was filled with the presence of another. A new life with unknown potential had been born into a softly lit room filled with gentle voices.

He barely cried but smiled, showing off his honest-to-goodness dimple. Then he was put on my stomach. He nursed happily as my placenta was delivered whole and intact. When he finished, he was content and ready to be held by his father.

My team started to disband, and soon our home was quiet and everyone, even baby, was asleep. Everyone, that is, except for me. I spent those early morning hours calling overseas in a voice filled with joy and happiness. Adrenaline is a wonderful thing. And then I told everyone that I had given birth at home. This saved me the aggravation of explaining myself beforehand. Mother and baby were fine and very happy. There was no rush to the hospital, no wondering where I would sleep. My baby and I spent the first of many nights cuddled up together in my own bed, safe and secure.

The next morning the children would come home and meet their new brother. My neighbor from across the hall would come and wonder how she hadn't heard a thing; my baby would nurse beautifully. But that was the next day. For now, I reveled in my birth and thanked God.

Mensch Tracht und Gott Lacht

Shaindel Tzadok

y baby's birth was, *baruch Hashem*, a tremendous lesson for our family in *hashgachah pratis*. On the one hand, we really felt HaKadosh Baruch Hu was leading us and caring for us in a very close way, and, on the other hand, He was showing us clearly that *"a mensch tracht und Gott lacht* — a man plans and God laughs."

I was due around Purim time, so when I started having contractions on Purim, I was very excited. They were still very light and far apart, so I decided to ignore them, although I told my oldest daughter (who was waiting impatiently for a Purim baby) that we might be having a baby today. We decided to go visit my grandmother, who lives in another neighborhood in Yerushalayim, all dressed up in costumes. We had a mini Purim party and had a great time.

As the afternoon wore on, the contractions started getting stronger and more regular, so the Purim celebration a day early (in Yerushalayim people celebrate the holiday on 15 Adar, Shushan Purim) was a welcome distraction. We left my grandmother at around 3:30 p.m. to be home in time to get ready for the megillah reading. I decided I had to make a cake since I was clearly in labor, and I had heard that it is a tremendous *segulah* for childless women to eat cake made by a laboring woman. Having no time to make anything elaborate, I made a plain white cake and some chicken and rice for dinner. I figured that wherever I would be that night the kids still had to eat.

Our excitement escalated as megillah time approached (although, other than the oldest and my husband, the family still knew nothing about the coming night's other event). We decided that I would take the middle children to hear megillah at the men's reading and the oldest would stay home with my three-year-old. She could hear megillah later at the reading for women, and if I had to go to the hospital, the kids would still have gotten to go to megillah with their mommy.

During the megillah reading active labor began, and I shifted in my chair, trying not to be noticeable. My eight-year-old daughter looked at me and said, "Ima, why are you so red?" I realized that I hadn't taken into account the longer "Hamans" when we decided to go to this reading. I told the children that if I left in the middle they should just stay until the end. They probably thought it was strange that I would suggest leaving during megillah, but they didn't ask any questions.

As soon as the megillah reading finished, we got up and ran out. It was a pouring, freezing Purim night, but we lived near the shul and we got home all right. I asked my husband to serve dinner — I couldn't do it by then. I was so cold and uncomfortable from sitting through megillah with strong contractions that I decided to go soak in the bath. As an afterthought, this was probably not the best idea since I was already in heavy labor. It was 8:00 p.m., and the hospital was more than twenty minutes away, but I was so uncomfortable that I wasn't being too prudent.

Soaking in a hot bath took the edge off the contractions, but soon that wasn't helping anymore. I also had the shakes, and I wasn't sure if I was cold or going into transition. I got out of the tub and got dressed quickly. When I came out, I just said to my husband, "Now!"

I told the kids we were going to the hospital, and they started to sing and dance around the room. In the meantime I went to call a cab. All the taxi companies either did not answer or said they had no cabs in our area and could not send one. We had no idea that Purim night was such a bad time to try to go to the hospital! As I hung up the phone from the last company's refusal, we realized we were really in a bind. We didn't own a car nor did we have any family in the area who had a car. All our friends with cars were busy Purim night, and we weren't looking forward to the attention that ordering an ambulance would attract.

Suddenly there was a knock on the door, and our personal "Eliyahu HaNavi" arrived! A relative of mine, who lives in a different neighborhood, has a son whose rebbe lives on our block. They came after megillah to wish their rebbe *a freilechen Purim*, but were told to come back in ten minutes. So they came to wish us *a freilechen Purim*.

My cousin works for an organization and sometimes has their car, which has a special blue siren that can be put on the roof when needed. This Purim he was working for them, so he came to us in a pickup truck, in the back of which someone had put a life-sized bear (in the spirit of Purim). We asked him if he could take us to the hospital right away.

He left his wife and son at our house with the younger kids and we got in. He looked at us and flew.

He had the siren and flashers on and, using the horn liberally, went through all the red lights. Due to the weather, there was very little traffic, *baruch Hashem*, but each bump was very hard for me.

At one point on the road we had to decide where to go. I had registered at both Hadassah Hospital in Har HaTzofim (Mount Scopus) and at Shaare Zedek Medical Center and had agonized over the decision of where to give birth. I have a medical condition that makes it important for me to deliver on my side and had just heard about a friend's wonderful experience giving birth this way in Har HaTzofim so I wanted to go there. On the other hand, America was expected to invade Iraq on that day, and I was afraid to be near Arabs on the day of a possible (God forbid) Arab-Israeli war. Har HaTzofim, although situated near a populated Jewish area, is located in East Jerusalem and therefore has many Arab patients. So, with a *tefillah* in our hearts, we went to Shaare Zedek.

We got to the hospital and rushed up to the delivery room. The admittance room, which is usually full, was empty that night. I was greeted by two English-speaking midwives. My Hebrew is good, but at such a time your native language is always reassuring. The midwife checked me and said I was nine and a half centimeters open and ready to go. I felt a need to go to the bathroom, but the midwife put her arm on my shoulder and in a motherly tone said, "*Bubbele*, you aren't going to any bathroom — let's go have this baby."

We walked into the delivery ward. I felt Hashem reassuring me when I saw a familiar face, a friend's mother-in-law who was a midwife at Shaare Zedek. She didn't know me, but seeing her face gave me a good feeling. I climbed up on the bed, ready to give birth. Now how would I convince the midwife to let me give birth in an unconventional position in a conventional hospital?

It turned out that the midwife assigned to me was the assistant head with tons of experience and an open outlook. I told her what I needed, and she said we could try it.

I had learned HypnoBirthing, so when it was time to push, I tried to use "breathing down" techniques instead of conventional Lamaze-type pushing. After about two contractions with no baby, the midwife said, "You have to push." No monitor, no IV — there was no time! With the next contraction I gave some hard, conventional-type pushes, and I guess that's the time Hashem set for my baby's birth, because after four hard pushing contractions the baby was out, with me in a side-lying position. "*Hodu laShem ki tov ki l'olam chasdo!*"

After the birth, my husband, who had been outside the reception room waiting to find out which delivery room I was being sent to, came in, only to see it was all over. We called our family and relatives, and then I was taken to the maternity ward. In the room, the woman in the other bed just nodded to me. I thought it was strange until I tried talking to her. She didn't know any Hebrew, only Arabic! A roommate I didn't want I got, and the delivery I thought I couldn't get, I got! *Mensch tracht und Gott lacht!*

Sterile Scissors

Rebbetzin Shaindel Bulman

When I was expecting my fourth child, we were living in the Catskill Mountains. It was three weeks after my due date, and a friend of mine had lent me a book entitled *Childbirth without Fear* by Grantly Dick-Read. Although I found it very interesting and enlightening, I returned it without having done any of the exercises.

I thought, *How long is this pregnancy going to go on? Enough is enough!*

I had a pile of laundry that I hadn't gotten around to because, for one thing, I was waiting for the new dryer to come and it was almost as late as the pregnancy itself. I seemed to remember that Dr. Read said something about squatting. So I attacked the laundry, squatting to pick up a shirt, standing to put it into the washing machine, squatting again to pick up a blouse, standing again to put it in the washing machine, until the machine was loaded. Then I added the detergent, started the machine, and sat down to rest.

That night I developed a nagging backache. I managed to sleep, waking only occasionally. Eventually it got stronger, finally waking me up early in the morning. I realized I was having contractions, and they were very close together. When I called the doctor to tell him, he said, "You will probably give birth today. You don't have to come to the hospital yet, but because it is snowing and may get worse, you should come soon."

Just before I put on my coat, I noticed some dirty dishes in the sink that had to be attended to. Who knew how long they would stay dirty if I didn't take care of them?

My husband asked, "Can anyone give birth with only mild pain?"

"Maybe a few lucky people," I answered, sure I had lots of time.

When we got to the hospital, a nurse came out, took one look at me, and ran to get a wheelchair. She took me straight to the delivery room, where she realized she had a problem. I was wearing a coat that had tight cuffs at the wrists. (They were called "mutton sleeves" because they fit tightly at the wrists but bellowed out at the arms.) Because of this, she couldn't get the coat off quickly enough. She decided to cut the sleeves with the only available scissors — the sterile ones.

I had barely gotten onto the table when the baby came swimming out. He had a veil pasted onto his face. I was told it was the membranes that hold the amniotic fluid. In order to get it off so he could start to breathe, they had to snip it behind the baby's ear to allow air to get under it. The only sterile scissors had been used to cut the coat. The nurse called up to the operating room upstairs to send scissors down quickly.

The scissors came in time for her to open the sac,

baruch Hashem. The only thing that was not quite right was his birth certificate. Instead of putting in the time of the baby's arrival, they put in twenty minutes later, the time of the doctor's arrival!

My VBAC Birth Adventure

Anna King

When contemplating one's life achievements, what would be on your list? Graduating college? Getting married? The birth of your first baby? For me, my VBAC (vaginal birth after cesarean) was one of the greatest achievements that stands out in my memory.

My first baby, although a great gift and blessing, had been born via C-section. It was a very traumatic experience for which I had not been prepared, and it took me many months to try to understand what had gone wrong and to reeducate myself for a better birth the next time. When my baby was nine months old, I became pregnant again. I was extremely concerned about how I would fare the second time around.

Two of the reasons recorded on my birth log for the C-section were "failure to progress" and the baby was big. For the next nine months, I read everything I could in order to ensure it would not happen again (unless, of course, there was no other way for my baby to be born healthy). Although some women do "fail to progress" and do have big babies, through my reading I learned that a large number of these women, if left alone, with no one staring at the clock, would labor until they had a safe birth. I felt I could be one of those women.

Many doctors are concerned when it comes to delivering a woman trying for a VBAC. They will try to discourage her with many scenarios, including uterine rupture, which can cause a woman to be left unable to become pregnant again, unnecessary labor, or even maternal or fetal death. I read the statistics for every scenario and spoke to many women who had had VBACs. Most importantly, I realized that the real strength was going to have to come from within me. I had to believe in myself.

I wrote a comprehensive birth plan, an outline of how I would like labor to progress if things were going well. I found a doula who was experienced and well respected in the hospitals. She would be my emotional and physical support. I also found out what were the policies of the hospital I had chosen to birth in. (This was very important, because one of the pitfalls we experienced was that the mildest pain relief methods we could have used was not available at the hospital.) I read up on what would increase my chances of a good birth experience and a successful VBAC. And, finally, I practiced putting myself in a state of relaxation where I could ride the contractions as if they were waves rather than working out how to stop the pain. Each wave would bring me closer to my goal, each one had a purpose, and I had to ride each one before my baby would be born.

On the night Sukkos was finished my body and soul

were ready, even though my due date had passed two weeks before. While my husband busied himself with disassembling the sukkah, I entertained a friend. By 1 a.m. she had won two rounds of Scrabble and, feeling satisfied, left me with a wish for a *"b'sha'ah tovah."* I sat with my husband for a drink and slice of cake before going to sleep when *wham*! my first real contraction hit.

I never finished my cake and drink, which was a funny reminder of my first birth, when I had come home to find forgotten tuna sandwiches still in the toaster oven because I had hastily run out. I called my doula, and she suggested I try to sleep. Well, my husband managed to sleep. I couldn't. I walked, paced, showered, and made sure everything was in my bag. At around 3 a.m. I woke my husband, needing some distraction. Later he also called my doula, who said she would come at around 5 a.m.

She was a welcome sight! My doula immediately helped relieve the pain through massage and breathing with me through contractions, all the while reminding me to eat and drink. Together we watched the sun come up over the mountains from my living room window. Labor was going according to plan, each contraction hopefully bringing me closer and closer to the moment I would meet my new baby.

By around 8 a.m. she thought it wise to go to the hospital. Maybe she picked up a difference in the length and frequency of the contractions. The car ride was very hard. We seemed to go over every bump in the road. Finally, after a quick run on the quiet weekend morning roads, we arrived at the hospital.

I was filled with anticipation of what would be. I had chosen the same hospital as before since my doula was well respected there and I would have more latitude there than in other hospitals. I was filled with dread as I was assigned a room and to a midwife who turned out to be the same one I had for my first baby. Was this a horrible twist of fate, to have labored so well at home only to face the same situation in the hospital as last time?

The nurse did some quick paperwork before assessing how far along I was. Expecting her to say I still had many hours and contractions left, I was in complete shock when she said, "Lady, you are nine and a half centimeters open!"

I started to shake and cry; I was so close to giving birth and to reaching my goal of a good VBAC. I remember asking if there was still a chance of me having a C-section, and she replied, "You will give birth very soon. Everything is going great."

Soon afterward I was told to push, although this time, unlike my first, I didn't need to be told! Great waves of contractions helped me push out my second baby girl in twenty minutes. She weighed even more than my first, and my doctor had said I couldn't give birth to my first baby, since she was so big (9 pounds 5 ounces). Now I had just given birth to an even bigger baby (9 pounds 7 ounces) fairly easily, with hardly any overwhelming contractions. I had never even thought to ask for pain relief. I hadn't failed to progress. I had labored at my own pace without constantly being berated for not dilating a certain amount by a certain time, like with my first. I had been surrounded with positive support, people telling me I could get through it. A lot of credit goes to my husband who had to put up with me for nine months with my nose always in a book, taking it out only to quote to him the latest statistics on VBAC.

As I sat holding my baby, I felt like jumping off the

bed and shouting to everyone, "I did it! I did it!" with thanks to Hashem for giving me the capability to give birth naturally. I was the happiest woman on the labor ward that day, feeling like I had turned birth, which had been such a bad experience, into one of the most meaningful points in my life.

> The author is a graphic artist but now has a special interest in childbirth education and women's health issues after her experiences. After her first VBAC she went on to have three more easy VBAC births! She has five beautiful girls, each born in their own unique way.

The Ambulance That Almost Made It

Estie Stillman

My husband, Shmuel, woke up at six that morning to go to shul, trying to be quiet so I could get a bit more sleep. I was in the ninth month of my pregnancy, and it was getting difficult, with three weeks still to go. This being my first child, I really had time to pace myself to prepare for the upcoming event. I had lots of time to organize the house, bake for the *simchah*, and freeze dinners for after the birth.

I woke up feeling something wet on my bed. I had learned about waters breaking as one of the ways one goes into labor, but I thought it usually happened two weeks before the birth at most. I still had plenty of time to go! Now what? Who should I call first?

I called Shmuel on his cell phone. He hadn't started davening yet. He said he would daven quickly and then come home. There was no real hurry because I was barely feeling any contractions.

The Ambulance That Almost Made It

My mother, who was also my labor coach, was three miles away. *I'd better call her fast*, I thought, because with the early morning traffic she would need extra time to call a cab and get here. Her first birth, me, went really quickly. I was hoping the same would be true for my first birth.

Suddenly I started to feel an unusual pressure. I thought I really should be feeling this near the end of the labor. I called my mom to tell her. She immediately called my childbirth teacher and explained her own experience when she gave birth to me. She decided to call a local Jewish ambulance. It wasn't available so she called the general ambulance service. She warned me to unlock the door in case they had to get in. Bless her for thinking to tell me that because the pressure I told her I was feeling was not imaginary.

I asked Hashem to please help. *How does one give birth alone?* All I remembered was that the sheets should be clean and blankets for warmth were important. I had changed the linen the night before, and my duvet was on the bed. There must have been something else I forgot.

Where is the ambulance? Where is my husband? Where is my mother? I kept asking myself. More water was coming out. More pressure. This was the biggest test in *emunah* I ever had to go through.

Hashem, You are literally the only One who can help me went through my mind.

Where is the ambulance? Maybe they got stuck in traffic. My mom had called them at 6:55. Guess they had other calls more important than her's. *Okay, Hashem, if there was ever a time I needed You, it's now.* I took some deep breaths to keep myself calm.

And there he was. I guided my baby out onto the

bed, noticing that the cord was wrapped twice around his neck. I lifted it off, covered him with the duvet, and when I heard that first cough followed by a cry, all I could say was "Thank you, Hashem."

Calmness came over me — or was it shock? I was very overwhelmed, wanting to cry — from joy because he was out and from fear and sadness because I was still alone.

The ambulance came at 7:20, three minutes after the baby was born. Shmuel walked in two minutes later. The only thing that was missing now was a camera to take a picture of his face as he looked at the medics, his wife (me), and his new 5-pound son.

In Joy I Reap
Raizel Stern

I glance at my night table and the current stack of books cluttering it, the contents of which reflect the various stages of my life. As a college student, I read trendy philosophical books. When I adopted a religious lifestyle, my reading material changed accordingly. I began reading books on Jewish philosophy. About five years later, books on marriage joined the pile.

I assumed that parenting books would soon be added to my collection. Instead I spent many years surrounded by reading material of a very different nature: infertility. As the years passed, my collection grew to include books on adoption. But eventually, thank God, after twelve years of waiting, birthing books adorned my night table. My reading material has now progressed to include books on child care and parenting, reflecting my treasured new status as a mother.

Some challenges and conditions can be successfully hidden, but infertility is not one of them. Throughout the years, my friends were empathetic and caring, although I did not discuss with them my pain and frustration. I am now prepared to share some thoughts on the years that preceded the birth of my children to help others appreciate the miracle that is often taken for granted — that of bringing children into this world — and to help others with their pain as they wait for their prayers to be answered.

I was in my mid-twenties when I met my husband, and we were married three months later. Each passing month we looked for signs indicating that in nine months' time we would be parents. Little did we realize that our path to parenthood would be significantly longer and fraught with uncertainty. But it would be a road we traveled together, growing closer and giving each other moral support.

Maybe it was a premonition of difficult times ahead, but more likely it was just a natural step for someone of my somewhat anxious temperament, which motivated me to consult a gynecologist a few months after we were married. When I look back now, I realize that the treatment he prescribed was very minor league compared to what was to follow. However, it helped us to begin to face the issues of infertility.

Once he felt that he had gone as far as he could, the doctor recommended that we go to a clinic that specialized in fertility problems. We looked to a *rav* for guidance on whether I should go for a complete fertility workup. The *rav* was emphatic; we had not been married for long, and the time was not right to place myself in the category of the infertile. We followed the *pesak* of the *rav*. This was not the time to be challenged by the stresses of fertility treatment.

We think that we make all the decisions, but Hashem sets the stage and pulls the strings. Various factors converged, and we were now ready to enter the world of major-league fertility treatment. I would soon be entering into a new phase of my life, a phase where most of my emotional energy would be invested in fertility clinics, asking complicated *she'eilos*, going to support groups, and trying to maintain some level of normalcy.

My first trip to the fertility clinic stands out in my memory. I remember vividly walking away from the gynecologist's rooms down a brightly lit corridor to an infertility clinic. I had crossed into another realm, a little-known world where all the players were either infertile couples like us or medical personnel wishing to employ all their medical expertise to help us conceive.

Infertility is a great equalizer. Age, status, or finances have no bearing here. Each woman subjects herself to endless blood tests, hormone treatments, ultrasounds, and other invasive procedures. Her life revolves around this clinic, and she complies with the doctor's orders, even if they may be uncomfortable. Daily visits to the clinic become the norm, and life becomes an emotional roller coaster. Do we dare hope that the next treatment will be successful? How do we deal with reality when the caring staff informs us that success has eluded us yet again? How do we protect ourselves and give each other encouragement when the months roll into years?

The earlier years were in a sense more painful; our hopes were high and the disappointments cut deeper. As the years progressed, we developed better coping skills, but the pain never left. Somehow we pushed ourselves to continue treatments, even though they were extremely stressful and the chances of success were decreasing with each subsequent treatment.

Each woman copes with the stress of treatment and infertility in different ways. I was not interested in the medical aspects of the treatments. Divorcing myself from my body was one of my major coping mechanisms. I did as I was told and kept as busy as possible, trying to ensure that there was never time to dwell on our childlessness. I tried to avoid situations that would be painful. I didn't hang around the park before the Shabbos afternoon ladies' *shiur*.

When is the time to give up and say it was just not meant to be? How much disappointment can one bear? Do we continue, somewhat resigned to the fact that all our efforts may possibly be in vain? Do we ask what are the chances of success? Are statistics important?

Entering the "over thirty-five" category was particularly difficult. Was there still room for hope? Should I let that depress me? All we needed was one successful fertilized egg to grow into the miracle of life. Was it ever meant to be? What should we be doing? Who should we turn to for a blessing? Can you follow up on every *segulah* that well-meaning people recommend? Even though I am not a "*segulah* person," I sat on a certain chair in Ashdod, prayed at the grave of a childless washerwoman, and followed some other recommendations provided by well-wishers. I had a friend set up a *shemiras halashon* rota when we were having a treatment. We davened constantly to HaKadosh Baruch Hu.

At the same time, we looked into adoption. We went to discuss the issue of adoption with a *rav* who we are close to. He said we should speak to a famous *rav* in Bnai Brak. The *rav* gave my husband a *berachah* and said we should adopt only a Jewish child and we should continue treatment. I very much wanted to adopt through a certain agency, but there were no Jewish babies.

It must have been difficult for our parents and siblings to see us in this trying situation. I appreciated my sister-in-law calling personally and telling me she was pregnant, although it must have been very uncomfortable for her. They knew we were having treatments, but we didn't tell them specifics or even the dates of the first nine procedures. I think we wanted to spare them the pain of disappointment. It was easier for us to cope on our own without having to deal with their disappointment, too.

Our friends were supportive, even though they could not fully understand what we were going through. I especially appreciated the fact that they treated me as a normal person and not someone who had to be treated with kid gloves. They always included us in family activities, and we chose what we felt comfortable to join in.

The challenge was answering innocent questions posed by strangers, such as "How many children do you have?" I felt worse for the person asking than for myself. I would spend the next fifteen minutes explaining that it is a natural question, and they had not hurt me by asking it. The more meaningful reaction was the countless number of people who said that they would daven for us. The only social situation that was really stressful was being *kvater* at a bris (a *segulah* for childlessness). However, we never passed this up.

After successive treatments failed, alternative treatments of questionable halachic status were suggested, but, of course, we could not accept them. We felt we were at an impasse.

One day a former student of mine said to me, "You must meet my uncle." She explained that her uncle, a respected Torah scholar, was an expert on fertility treatments. Her words came at a time when we were dealing with the reality of stopping treatments. Should I make the call? Could he really help us?

Later that evening my husband and I found ourselves sharing our medical history with a distinguished-looking man clad in rabbinic garb. His manner was both professional and caring as he asked for medical details. Then he declared, "You may think you are young, you may even look like you are young, but your body is not."

I was thirty-seven years old at the time. He proceeded to outline for us exactly what we should do and what particular procedure should be used. He told us that he would make all the initial appointments. Something in his manner compelled us to follow his directives. He followed the case, calling me and supervising our progress.

Who was this man, and why was he so devoted to my case? Apparently he had amassed information on fertility, possibly based on his own personal experience, and he genuinely felt the pain of a couple going through this challenge. He felt it was a sacred obligation to do all he could to assist countless couples on their quest.

Everything was different with this treatment. We were at a new clinic in a different city. My husband accompanied me on every visit. This wasn't necessary in previous treatments. Also, this time we told family and close friends that we were having a treatment. I set up my own *mishmeres* of *shemiras halashon*.

A special atmosphere permeated the shul that Rosh HaShanah. No doubt everyone had something to pray for. I davened as I had never davened before. Just the previous day I had undergone yet another procedure under the direction of my new clinic. On a medical level chances were slim. But I had just spent the month of Elul learning at a women's seminary and felt spiritually ready for Rosh HaShanah. I felt that this time my prayers might be answered. Was there a possibility of success this time? I turned my energy upward and appealed to Hashem, the All-Merciful One.

The days passed slowly, and we found ourselves in the familiar situation of awaiting the results of the pregnancy test, praying for success but also bracing ourselves for disappointment. The minutes dragged. Part of me wished that time could be sped up and we could phone immediately. Another part wished that time could be frozen so that we would not have to face another disappointment. This was our tenth treatment. We had invested so much in this one.

Before the appointed time, the phone rang. My husband answered, immediately recognizing the voice of the nurse. She asked for me and then pronounced the long-awaited words, "You're pregnant!"

I had hoped and prayed for this day for over a decade, not knowing whether I would ever arrive at this point.

My life shifted into a different gear. Caution was in order and I was told to take it easy. And take it easy, I did. I arranged for the best in medical care, as well as attending birthing classes. When I was twelve days past my due date, it became apparent that a C-section was required. I was also informed that if I didn't do it that day, I would have to wait two more days.

Honestly, I was so ready emotionally to have this baby. Others may have done it differently, but I didn't want to wait any longer, and I didn't really want to go through labor at this point. I was thirty-eight years old and just wanted to see my baby.

So on a pleasant summer day, a few months after our twelfth anniversary, we were blessed with a most beautiful baby boy. It is impossible to describe our elation. My husband called everyone we knew all over the world. I could not sleep for a week. I wanted to hold the baby all the time. I had to make sure he was safe. The hospital staff was understanding, allowing me to ignore the standard routines.

I set aside my normally reserved demeanor, and I proceeded to share my good news with everyone. This, together with the surgery, lack of sleep, and the endless discussions about "The Bris," were all very emotionally draining.

The bris was very moving, with family, friends, and colleagues participating as if our *simchah* were their own.

When my son was six months old, I began thinking of the possibility of having another child. I didn't want him to be an only child. But dare I ask Hashem for another miracle?

Motivated by my desire for my son's happiness, I contacted the clinic again. Again we proceeded with treatments, but my whole state of mind was different. I did not come home to an empty house after each visit. I came home to a gurgling baby, happy to see me. Although the stress level was lower, the roller coaster of emotions began again. Could it possibly work? I was older, but I had successfully carried and given birth to a live baby. I appreciated the doctor's honesty when he did not give me any false hope.

Again the day arrived, and we waited anxiously for the results of the pregnancy test. There was no early phone call. Definitely a negative result. We waited patiently for the designated phone time. With trembling hands I called, surprising my doctor, who answered the phone. I told him who was calling, and he said, "*Mazel tov.*" We could not believe the *chesed* of Hashem. Another miracle!

I could not take it easy this time; I had an energetic baby to take care of. Thanks to him I went into the second C-section in much better physical shape than the first. I thought of names for my son's soon-to-be playmate and began to plan a bris, assuming that it would be another boy. Imagine our elation when we were blessed with a beautiful little girl to complete our family.

Now, five years later, I try to be constantly appreciative of my precious treasures and try to never take them for granted. I aim to be the perfect parent and feel guilty when I am not. Being an older parent has lots of pluses and challenges, but I am grateful for the way our children have changed our lives.

We are also extremely grateful for the many medical professionals as well as family and friends who were always there for us. One nurse was particularly caring, making herself available whenever I needed her. She helped me with all my medical needs, but was also a source of tremendous emotional support. Her strong *emunah* and *bitachon* gave me the courage to cope with the treatment. I value her friendship to this day.

How has my whole experience affected me? Although I would have never chosen this path, I see how our marriage and we ourselves have grown from our challenges. I try to have greater sensitivity to others going through difficult times.

We continue to see the hand of Hashem guiding us in all aspects of our lives and our children. We are eternally grateful to Him for our twofold treasure. We pray that we will be able to raise our children to be a true *ben* and *bas Yisrael.*

Generally I don't dispense advice. However, since I have crossed the bridge and am now a mother, women have asked me to give them suggestions of what to say to a neighbor, friend, or relation who is childless. This is what I tell them:

- There is no magic formula for what is right for everybody, and even if you say the right thing you may say it at the wrong time.
- If you can, try to include them in your life, but give them space for their privacy. I have learned that you can have a close, supportive relationship with someone even if you don't share intimate information.
- Try to understand where the person is in terms of how they relate to your children. It is wonderful if a natural bond develops, but you can't force it.
- Don't tell your children not to ask where their children are. It is natural for children to ask. If it is difficult for the person to answer, tell your children that they should daven that soon this person will be a mommy.
- If you notice, I was the one who was getting all the support. There are two members in a couple; husbands need support, too. This is more complicated because in general men don't seek or give emotional support the way women intuitively do. Invite the couple over and try to encourage your husband to develop a friendship. It is unlikely that the husband will discuss anything related to the infertility, but he will appreciate the warmth of a friendship.

What I would suggest to childless couples:

- Find a *rav* whom you are prepared to follow and who is as knowledgeable as possible concerning aspects of infertility treatments. When you ask a *she'eilah*, make sure you present all the relevant information.
- If you choose the medical route, find the best medical treatment available.
- Look for support groups. Other people are a source of important information.
- Try to give yourself and your husband mechanisms for coping when things get rough, as they do. Pamper yourselves. Go out for dinner.
- Don't feel obliged to share what you are going through, but if you can find the right person, it helps.
- Prepare tactful answers for insensitive questions. Don't let yourself get hurt by tactless comments. Judge these people favorably; they have no means of understanding the depth of your pain.
- Avoid situations that are painful, but don't exclude yourself from society.
- Be a source of support for one another.
- Daven, having *emunah* that your prayers will be answered.
- Do all the *hishtadlus* necessary, physical as well as spiritual. Slim, healthy women have a higher chance of fertility being successful.
- Don't put your life on hold. See yourself as a whole person waiting for your little *pikadon* to be delivered.

Ladies' Room Birth

*As told to Rebbetzin Shaindel Bulman
by a woman in a taxi*

Contractions had come so suddenly and strong that by the time she reached the hospital all she wanted to do was use the ladies' room. Once there, she realized that it wasn't the facilities she needed but the doctor! She didn't feel she had waited too long at home. It had just come on so quickly.

She screamed to her husband to bring help. He didn't know which way to go. He didn't feel right about leaving her alone, but he didn't want to deliver the baby either. It is amazing how much strength a woman has when she has to. Hashem was with her. She let out a scream. *"Help!"*

The pressure became overwhelming, and she knew this was it. She let go and thought, *If this is what's meant to be, then so be it*. Out came a baby boy, pink as anything, He cried almost immediately, as if to say, "A bathroom? What a place to be born."

Her husband returned with a nurse. Someone else was running after them with a wheelchair. Wheelchair?

She was beyond needing wheelchair assistance. They brought a gurney to wheel her to the birthing floor as another assistant wrapped and accompanied them with her new son.

She was much calmer after being inside the (real) delivery room, and her husband began to make calls.

Her parents were waiting anxiously to know if they should book their tickets for a bris. Her mom would come in any case.

The doctor went out to her husband to tell him there were complications and to wait before making the calls. Now her husband started to pace the floor. He called his rebbe for a *berachah*.

A few minutes later the doctor returned saying, "*Mazel tov*! It's a girl!"

"What do you mean?" asked her husband. "It's a boy!"

"Yes," said the doctor, "and also a girl."

The "complication" the doctor had spoken of was bleeding after the delivery of her son, which is normal. When he first came in to check her, they hadn't told him she had already given birth.

Her parents did indeed come for the double *simchah* — a bris and a *kiddush*.

No Surprises, Please!

Ahuva Steinmetz

As an avid reader, I prepared for my upcoming (first) birth by reading no less than five books on pregnancy and childbirth. By the time my ninth month arrived, I knew just about everything a layperson needs to know about the various stages of childbirth. One of my coworkers, a mother of eight, expressed her surprise at my eagerness to learn so much about childbirth in advance. But I try to approach every new experience armed with as much information as possible. No surprises, please!

I practiced breathing and relaxing, prepared a list of things to take to the hospital, and began freezing meals in anticipation of the big day. Still, there was a lot left to be done. I remember feeling rather overwhelmed one Sunday, almost three weeks before my due date, as I tried to plan my activities for the coming week. My obstetrician had gone out of town suddenly (her mother-in-law had passed away), so I had to reschedule my appointment with her. I also had to register at the hospital, pack my hospital bag, get hold of a few emergency numbers, borrow a carriage or bassinet, and shop for a stroller. There were only three weeks left; how would I fit everything in?

I soon learned that my plans were not in my hands, after all.

When I went to sleep that night, I suddenly felt a gush of liquid. It took me a few minutes to realize what it was. I crept out of bed and ran for my favorite book on childbirth, hoping my husband, who had just drifted off to sleep, wouldn't notice anything. What if I was just imagining things?

If I had understood the book correctly, I wasn't imagining things. My heart pounding, I woke up my husband, Uri, who was as surprised as I was by this turn of events. My fingers trembled as I called up my labor coach, Mrs. Furster, to ask her what we should do next.

"Are you having contractions?" she asked, completely undisturbed by the fact that it was already 12:30 a.m.

"No." I didn't feel a thing, not even more fluid.

"Since you're early and your baby is small, it's probably best for you to go to the hospital to be examined."

My doctor had sent me for an ultrasound a few weeks before to determine whether my baby was developing properly, since by her estimation he seemed quite small. *Baruch Hashem*, he was developing well, but he was only about 5 pounds, probably due to my digestive difficulties over the course of the pregnancy.

"Give me a few minutes to get dressed," Mrs. Furster continued. "I'll give you a call when I'm ready to go, and then we'll meet at the hospital."

I thanked her, hung up the phone, and told Uri, "Quick, we need to get ready to go."

This isn't really happening, is it? I asked myself as I got dressed. *I still have three weeks to go.* I had actually assumed I'd be a little bit late, since most of my mother's births were a week after her due date. Besides, everyone said first babies were normally late. I wasn't ready yet!

My baby, and Hashem, had apparently deemed that I was ready. Uri and I quickly packed some basics, not knowing how long we'd be in the hospital. I didn't have time to pack everything on my carefully prepared list, so I quickly gathered the essentials — water, food, books to read, robe, slippers, money, phone numbers.

As soon as Mrs. Furster called to say she was ready, Uri called a taxi. We were at the hospital in record time, and we sat down in the lobby to wait for Mrs. Furster. It only took her about ten minutes to come, but to me it seemed like forever. I was shivering, trying to stay calm. Uri said later I did a good job because he would have been much more nervous if I hadn't been so calm.

Mrs. Furster accompanied me to the examining room, while Uri stayed outside. I was hooked up to a monitor and examined. Yes, my waters had broken, and I was actually having mild contractions. I was already three centimeters dilated.

Wow, this is great, I thought. First births were reputed to drag on forever; some women take hours just to dilate three centimeters.

It was so nice to have Mrs. Furster there. We chatted easily while the monitor did its job. Though the hospital regulations require registering in advance of the birth, the nurse at the desk processed my papers and registered me on the spot. Mrs. Furster answered her questions about my age, physical condition, and medical history.

"Do you have another doctor you want to call?" Mrs. Furster asked when I told her that my obstetrician was out of town.

"I guess not," I said a little uneasily. We were planning to get the numbers of some backups ready, but we hadn't had a chance.

When it was confirmed that my waters had broken, I was admitted to the hospital, and Mrs. Furster went out to apprize Uri of the situation. He was very excited, smiling from ear to ear when I met him in the delivery room after changing into the hospital gown Mrs. Furster gave me. You would think she was a member of the hospital staff!

The hospital was very quiet, which was great. I had specifically chosen it because I didn't want to give birth in a crowded, busy place. There was only one other woman in the delivery ward when I came, and she gave birth soon after I settled into my room. For the rest of the night, I had the place to myself.

The nurse who was assigned to me hooked me up to the monitor in my delivery room and to an IV. She asked if I wanted some Demerol to soften my cervix and get my labor moving a little.

I was in no rush. By this time it was about two o'clock, and I was exhausted. "Can I sleep a little first?"

"Okay," she said.

I lay down in the bed and tried to make myself comfortable. Mrs. Furster and Uri sat down in the two chairs in the room. I was still hardly feeling my contractions, so I figured I could get a little sleep before things progressed. I was too excited to sleep, though. *Who would have thought I'd be in the hospital so soon! I can't wait to call Mommy in the morning... I wonder if it will be a boy or a girl.*

My husband is the oldest of four boys, and my in-laws were convinced we'd have the first girl in the family. Uri, however, was looking forward to having a boy, and I didn't want to disappoint him, though I wouldn't have minded a girl myself. We had already picked out two names, and I knew Uri really wanted a son to name after his grandfather, who had passed away when he was in high school.

"Can you sleep?" Uri whispered to me after a little while.

"No," I whispered back.

"Mrs. Furster is sleeping."

"She told me she was in the hospital all day with another woman."

At four o'clock, the nurse came in to examine me again. I was four centimeters dilated, and I had begun to feel the contractions, though they were not too uncomfortable. Again, she offered me Demerol or Pitocin to move things along. Mrs. Furster had explained that once a woman is admitted to the hospital, the staff is eager for things to progress, which is why normally she helps women labor at home for as long as possible. But in my case, since my waters had broken and my baby was early, there hadn't been much of a choice.

"I'd rather not take any medication yet," I told the nurse.

Mrs. Furster spoke up. "It might be a good idea. Since you haven't been able to sleep, you could be too worn out to push when it's time."

The last point made a lot of sense to us. Uri and I discussed the situation and decided that I should take some pitocin. The nurse added it to my IV drip, and within a few minutes the contractions got a little stronger.

For a while I was able to distract myself by reading. Mrs. Furster recommended that Uri go daven *shacharis* at a *vasikin minyan* before things became more exciting, and off he went.

Soon I was no longer able to ignore the contractions.

We weren't timing them because the monitor was taking care of that. Mrs. Furster reminded me not to fight the contractions, just to let them do their job. That helped a lot.

At about six o'clock the nurse unhooked me from the monitor for a few minutes. I thought I'd walk around the hospital a bit, like the books recommended, but Mrs. Furster suggested that we use the time to daven *shacharis*. I put on my robe and davened an abridged *shacharis*, but I found it quite difficult to concentrate, especially when a contraction came.

Before the nurse hooked me back up to the monitor, I borrowed Mrs. Furster's cell phone to call my mother. She's an early riser, so I knew she'd be awake. She was very excited to hear from me and said she'd come visit in a couple of hours.

Since my contractions were still coming very irregularly, and I was only four and a half centimeters dilated, the nursed upped my pitocin dosage. Uri returned from davening to find me breathing my *1-2-3!* breaths through each contraction. A new nurse came on duty at seven and examined me. I was only five and a half centimeters dilated. It didn't disturb me too much, but the nurse offered me Demerol (again!). I said no (again), determined to see how far I could go without any pain relievers.

Finally the contractions began coming more frequently and with greater intensity. I worked on my breathing, surprised at how much it helped. Mrs. Furster massaged my back, while Uri provided encouragement. In between contractions, I said *tehillim*, again at Mrs. Furster's suggestion. Although I'd heard that labor is an *eis ratzon* and a good time to daven for other people, I didn't have the presence of mind for that.

At 8:15, I suddenly felt the urge to push. Mrs. Furster called the nurse, who determined that I was already fully dilated — incredible progress for just an hour and a quarter! *Don't first births take forever?* I wondered. (Uri told me later that sometime during that hour and a quarter I was given some more pitocin without my knowledge. However, even Mrs. Furster said she didn't expect things to move along that fast.)

My mother arrived just then, but I asked that she stay out of the room — I didn't want anyone else around while I gave birth. I'd heard that pushing is the easiest part of labor, but for me it was the scariest and most difficult step. I tried to stay calm and listen to the instructions issued by Mrs. Furster and the nurse. In my mind, I prayed for Hashem's help.

It took half an hour for the baby to descend, but I didn't notice the time passing at all. I was hyperventilating and fighting the urge to panic. Suddenly his head came out, and then I felt the nurse freeing his shoulders, and the rest of his body slipped out.

It was a boy! They laid him on my chest, all covered with white gook, and he screamed and screamed. I tried to comfort him for a minute, unable to believe that it was all over. Then the nurse took him to clean him up, weigh him, and dress him. Although he was small — only five and a half pounds — everything was in perfect working order.

My husband got to hold the baby while the placenta was delivered and the staff doctor stitched me up. *Baruch Hashem*, I didn't need an episiotomy, even though it's sometimes routine for first births, and I hardly tore. I only needed a few internal stitches, which Mrs. Furster assured me do not hurt as much as external ones.

Finally, the stitching was done, and my mother came into the room. She helped me try to nurse the baby while Uri went to call his parents. Mrs. Furster left, too, happy that all had gone well but exhausted after a full day and night on duty.

I was full of adrenaline and could not believe my good fortune. A beautiful, healthy little boy, so much sooner than I had anticipated! My mother, a first-time grandmother, was equally excited.

The baby wasn't interested in nursing, so eventually I surrendered him to the nurse, who took him to the nursery.

Things quieted down a little at that point. My mother left, promising to be back that afternoon during hospital visiting hours. I was allowed to stay in the delivery room for another hour or so before the nurse moved me to the maternity ward. Unlike my poor husband, I was wide awake. Who could be tired after such an exciting event?

True, things hadn't gone exactly as I had planned — I had been expecting the somewhat slower natural labor process, free of medication. As far as surprises go, though, it turned out terrific. I am extremely grateful to Hashem that I had such a smooth, complication-free birth, that I was able to handle the pain, that I stayed calm almost the entire time, that Mrs. Furster was there to help from the beginning to the end, and that I have a wonderful, healthy baby. I can only pray that my future births go as easily!

> *Editor's note*: Depending on the situation, induction (where pitocin is administered to start labor) or augmentation (where pitocin is used to speed up labor) is not always advisable. Many studies show it can lead to complications (though other studies show no difference

> in outcome). Studies show that infection may not increase with time lapse from waters breaking to delivery, but rather from the time of the first internal exam until delivery as well as frequency and quantity of internal examinations. Medical safety is the priority, but when weighing equal options, the birthing mom's physical and emotional needs should be taken into consideration as well (*American College of Obstetrics and Gynecology*, "Induction of labor," Practice bulletin, no. 10; *JAMA*, Statistical bulletin (Jan. 21, 1998); Hannah, ME, et. al., *New England Journal of Medicine*, "Induction of Labor Compared with Expectant Management for PROM at Term" (1996), 334 no. 10: 1005–10).

In for a Landing

Devorah

I was a bit apprehensive about the birth of my sixth child. The previous five had all been born in a small birthing hospital, known for its open-minded and natural approach to childbirth. But that hospital had recently closed its doors, and I was forced to find a new venue. I seriously considered a home birth, but we live too far away from a hospital if, God forbid, something were to go wrong.

I decided on the large teaching hospital that was close to our home. Its approach was reportedly the most natural of the alternatives in our city. About a month before my due date I went for a tour. The midwife who gave me the tour extolled the virtues of the hospital and its natural approach — allowing the laboring woman to use the shower, a beanbag chair, various positions, and even a mirror to allow her to watch the birth. I asked the midwife if I would be allowed to bring in a birthing stool. I had birthed my third and fourth babies on a birthing stool. They were beautiful births.

The midwife actually seemed excited about the idea.

After the tour we spoke to the head midwife about it, but she did not agree. I had also been informed by that time that a heparin lock was standard hospital procedure. I had never been jabbed at any of my previous births, and I wasn't looking forward to it now.

That night, after coming home from the tour, I phoned my labor coach. Half-jokingly, half-seriously, I said that I wished I could just walk around the hospital lobby until I was ready to push. Little did I know how prophetic those words would be.

Three days before my due date I went to the homeopathic pharmacy to buy Caulophyllum, which is known to promote smooth, steady contractions. My labor coach had given it to me during the birth of my fourth child. The pharmacist suggested that I take one dose three to four times a day and then every two hours when in active labor. I had also been drinking herbal tea during my last trimester, as I had during my previous pregnancies — three cups per day of red raspberry leaf combined with nettles. They provide calcium, magnesium, iron, and other elements, toning the uterus and making for a potentially healthier pregnancy and easier labor.

About midday on my due date, I lost my mucous plug. Contractions hadn't begun yet, but I started getting excited, knowing that my baby would soon arrive. I tried to stay active during the rest of the afternoon, so I took the children to the park, pushed them on the swings, and then ran home (well, walked) to get some drinks and snacks.

At around five or six in the afternoon I became aware of the contractions. I started getting antsy, and my older children knew that something was up. I retired to my bedroom for some quiet where I could focus. By eight in the evening the contractions were regular, about fifteen minutes apart. I phoned my labor coach to let her know where I was holding. My husband put the children to sleep while I took a long, relaxing shower. I crawled into bed thinking that if tonight was going to be the night, it would do me good to get some rest. If this wasn't the real thing, then lying down would stop the contractions and I would have a good night's sleep, ahead of tomorrow's ordeal.

At ten-thirty, I was still awake and still having contractions. By eleven they were ten minutes apart. I got out of bed, went downstairs and tidied up the kitchen, and prepared myself a thermos full of raspberry leaf and nettles tea to take to the hospital.

By now I was breathing and swaying through my contractions. I like to remain upright during labor; I think that gravity helps the baby move down the birth canal.

My husband came downstairs at around midnight, sensing that something was up. I told him to get ready — tonight was the night. We got our things together (I still hadn't packed my bag), phoned the labor coach, and our friend who had volunteered to come over and stay with the children.

There are two roads that lead from our house to the hospital — the main highway, which is fairly straight, well lit, and takes about forty-five minutes, and the mountain road, which is dark, curvy, and takes about twenty-five minutes. My husband said that due to the late hour, we should go via the highway.

Just before leaving for the hospital, I had the keen sensation that if we didn't leave now, the baby was going to be born right then and there. I rushed to the car. "We'd better take the mountain road," I told my husband. I did not want to have my baby in the car.

Cellular phones are an amazing invention. I was on the phone with my labor coach during most of the car ride. She spoke to me in such a calm, relaxing voice and helped me breathe through the contractions. They were coming about every two minutes now. We picked up my coach at the front gate of the hospital and continued on to the emergency room — after midnight the labor ward is only accessible by entering through the emergency room.

While my husband parked the car, my coach helped me meander through the long hallways and down the stairs in order to get to the labor room. "Why do laboring women have to go downstairs?" I thought aloud. I was also worried that my husband would never find us in this maze of a hospital. Luckily it had signs, but I was too far gone to notice them.

When we got to the labor ward, I suggested to the midwife that she skip the initial prep and we go straight to the delivery room. I guess, after looking at my face, she knew I was right.

The midwife escorted us into the delivery room, and my coach helped me change into a hospital gown. The midwife then asked me to get up on to the bed to be checked. At that stage, it looked like a feat second only to climbing Mount Everest. Somehow, in between contractions, I managed. I was on all fours now, breathing through contractions, which were coming one right on top of the next. The midwife wanted me to turn over onto my back.

"I can't," I cried. "Can't you find another midwife who can check me this way?" My coach was great, calming me down and explaining that this was the quickest, easiest way that they know how to check. Somehow I managed to roll over onto my left side.

"Fully dilated," said the midwife.

I was relieved.

Just then a fifty-something salt-and-pepper-haired doctor stuck his head in the doorway. I had never had a doctor present at any of my previous births, and I didn't need or want to start now. "Have her waters broken?" he asked.

"No," answered the midwife.

"Then why don't you break them?" suggested the doctor.

"You don't need to break my waters," I called out.

This was not the natural birth I had dreamed about. After another minute, I noticed that the contractions had stopped and that I was in a bit of a lull. I had read that this sometimes happens before the pushing stage, but I had never experienced it before. I mentioned it to my coach. She was very encouraging.

I think that at about this time the midwives were trying to get me hooked up to an IV and maybe even a monitor (standard hospital procedure, remember?). They never succeeded, though. I don't even remember the contraction coming on, but all of a sudden, without thinking about it, my body took over. I flipped over onto all fours, took a deep breath, and started pushing. I gave one big push and my waters broke; the baby's head followed.

"She's pushing, and she's not stopping," one midwife called out to the other.

Another push and the body slipped out. "It's a boy!" I cried, elated.

The midwife handed me my son, and I held him close. I wasn't sure if she had caught him or if he had landed on the bed; it all happened so fast. My coach remembers him landing on the bed, saying I had maneuvered my back close to the bed for the "landing" while the midwife was putting on her second glove.

I sat up in the bed, cuddling and nursing my baby for about twenty minutes before delivering the placenta. Somehow, without my noticing it, the midwife managed to hook me up to the IV and was administering a dose of pitocin to help my uterus contract and to prevent hemorrhaging. I had never needed this before, but this was "standard hospital procedure" for a sixth birth. It no longer mattered — fifteen minutes after arriving at the hospital, I was holding my healthy baby boy in my arms.

> *Editor's note*: Caregivers are learning more about various positions for labor and delivery. Don't be shy to try what feels most comfortable for you.

Two Sisters, Two Births

Yehudis Feller

A month had passed since we moved back to Pennsylvania. We'd spent a year in Israel so my husband could strengthen his learning. It was a wonderful chance for us, a newly married couple, to get to know each other and connect in a special Torah environment. I must admit, it also added some excitement and adventure to the start of our marriage.

I was even luckier because my sister had moved there the year before, and she and her husband decided to stay. Before I even arrived, a place had been rented for me. She knew what I was looking for, something close to her and not far from the *kollel*. Other than that, I wasn't fussy.

My sister and I had a wonderful time together, meeting new people while keeping in touch with the old. Our relationship also took on a new facet because we were becoming first-time moms together. We compared notes about our pregnancies, me with my nausea, her with her shortness of breath. She was three months ahead of me so she shared the childbirth books she had bought, and we decided to take a childbirth course together. We were both interested in a nonmedicated birth, but we wanted someone who was balanced as our teacher. Things don't always work out the way you expect. I have heard enough stories to know that.

We finished our course, feeling as prepared as possible. The class on cesarean birth was the only one we didn't really pay attention to. It was a hot day, and Dinah spent the time dozing. We both thought, *It isn't going to be me.*

Dinah was giving birth in Jerusalem, so there was no problem with her going into labor the day after the course finished. She was in her thirty-eighth week. It was especially nice that I was feeling fine and was there to help her. I was scheduled to leave in just under two months — we were going to my mom for Pesach. There, in Scranton, Pennsylvania, I would have the baby.

An Unexpected Turn of Events

Dinah called me to come one Thursday to help her around the house. She thought something was starting and wanted to clean up for Shabbos. I went home at about ten o'clock.

Dinah had labored most of the night, becoming more tired as the hours wore on. She didn't call me until the early morning because she tried breathing and visualizing on her own for some time even before she woke up her husband. Dinah wanted to feel the connection to her baby, trying to help herself bring her baby down, before anyone else would assist her. It was a special, private time of introspection. She said it was a time to connect spiritually, too.

As the contractions strengthened and became

closer, Dinah woke up her husband. He was impressed when she told him she had been up for almost six hours in labor. As he calmly breathed with her, timed contractions, and helped her with other tricks she had learned in her class to help her through labor, they both knew that soon it would be time to go. Then Dinah called me to tell me she wouldn't be coming that night for Shabbos. I came over to help.

With her contractions coming three to four minutes apart, we decided to go to the hospital. She called her doctor, who met us there. When we got there, Dinah was hooked up to the monitor, and we found out she was four centimeters dilated. We were a bit disappointed even though she was almost completely effaced; we thought she must be further along. Her doctor decided to stay a couple more minutes to see how the monitor looked before making her rounds. What a shock when the doctor saw that the baby was in distress. The heartbeat was dropping with each contraction and wasn't returning quickly enough.

The doctor gave Dinah oxygen, turned her on her left side, and waited through the next couple contractions. Nothing was helping.

The doctor, whom we trusted completely, said, "The baby's heartbeat is not returning to normal after a contraction." She explained patiently that Dinah would need a cesarean birth. Her baby was in distress and needed help. As Dinah was moved to the operating room, she was allowed to call her parents so they could daven for her. Afterward she told me she was given respect and treated with dignity as they prepared her for the surprise cesarean. Her shock and disappointment was lessened because of the support system around her.

They administered epidural anesthesia while the

OR staff was gathered. Lots of thoughts flashed through her mind: *Will my baby be healthy? Why is the heartbeat dropping? Will I be able to nurse?*

The doctor checked her again to see if she had dilated any more after the epidural had taken effect. Maybe there was still hope for a vaginal birth?

No, she was only five centimeters dilated, and the baby wasn't doing well. At 8:40 a.m., just under an hour after we arrived, Dinah gave birth to a baby girl weighing 5 pounds 8 ounces.

When they took the baby out, they saw that the cord was wrapped twice tightly around the baby's neck. That was why the baby had been in distress.

Dinah had done all that she could to see that her pregnancy and birth was a success; she ate well, exercised, hired a quality caregiver. Although Dinah knows she did all that she could, it was too soon to go over it to write it down for others. She is still up at nights a lot, successfully nursing the baby, and repeats to herself, *It was still a birth, just another way to exit.*

Another Cesarean?

Pesach was approaching. I flew to Scranton in my eighth month because my brother-in-law was getting married shortly after I was due, and we didn't want to miss the wedding. I had a doctor's appointment the week I arrived. When I had gone for an ultrasound in my fifth month, my baby had been breech. At that point, my doctor said it was pointless to even give it any thought because the baby was still moving a lot. I mentioned to the doctor in America that I was concerned that my baby might still be breech. He said he was sure he felt the head where it should be, but just to be safe, he sent me for an ultrasound. As I'd suspected, my baby was still head up.

He said to wait a couple of weeks before doing anything.

My sister called Rav Yisrael Yaakov Fisher because she'd heard he knew *segulah*s for this type of thing. He gave us instructions, which involved going to a natural spring of water. We searched maps, spoke to people who knew the surrounding area, and made phone calls to many springwater companies. Finally, we set out to one spring, but it was dried up, then to another one, but we couldn't find it. After literally hours of traveling and hiking, we returned home exhausted.

I called my sister, discouraged. She called my birthing consultant in Israel who suggested that I lie down with music and light where I want the baby to turn. Since babies can see and hear in utero, it can get them to change positions. This had worked for five out of six of her women, so I decided to try it. Unfortunately, it didn't work for me.

It was getting closer to my due date, and my baby was still not in the right position. My doctor spoke to me about doing a version, turning the baby around externally. The risk, he said, was that the baby might go into distress, and then I would certainly need a C-section. If my baby wasn't head down, I knew I'd need a C-section anyway, so I decided to go for it.

The day arrived, one and a half weeks before my due date. In the hospital they hooked me up to an IV, and I lay there with my husband by my side, connected to a monitor for an hour before they'd start the procedure. They did an ultrasound to make sure there was enough fluid and the cord was okay.

The doctor attempted to turn the baby three times. Each time my baby flipped back after having reached the midpoint. It was fascinating to watch, even though I was anxious about the lack of success.

The doctor couldn't do it. Once again I was connected to the monitor for an hour before going home to make sure the baby was all right.

Now we had to discuss our other option — a C-section. We decided that at my next appointment we would schedule one. My sister called my birth counselor again. She said that for a variety of reasons it could be better to wait until one goes into labor to have a cesarean. My husband and I decided to wait.

Six days before my due date, I heard that one of my friends had two versions done successfully by a specialist in New York. Within minutes I had him on the phone, explaining my situation. The next day I was in his office in the ultrasound room. He tried to turn the baby once, twice. Nothing. I was too tense. My last hope was to have the baby turned after an epidural in the operating room. In case of a problem during the procedure, he would do a caesarian.

We ran to the pay phone and started calling doctors and *rabbanim*. After a couple of hours, which seemed like years, we decided to do it. Did I have another choice?

A Beautiful Birth

I was very scared and nervous but so grateful that my husband was allowed into the operating room with me. When they came to administer the epidural, the anesthesiologist entered along with an intern with an Arab-sounding name. This only added to my anxiety. An Arab and an intern as well. But it actually went quickly and smoothly. I felt a little pressure, then cold, and it was over.

The doctors left. As I lay there, I started losing feeling in my legs. The nurses came and tried to keep me calm. They were so nice and helpful throughout. The doctor returned and started feeling around my stomach while making friendly conversation. After two minutes he turned to my husband and me and said, "Thank God it worked. Everything's all right." He had distracted us in conversation, all the while turning the baby!

I was examined, and I was three centimeters dilated. Maybe I had been having mild contractions for a couple of hours and hadn't noticed? So, instead of walking out of the operating room and driving home, I was to give birth in a hospital far from home. They wouldn't discharge me if I was already dilating, so they moved me to a birthing room, and I braced myself for what was to come.

It was late and I was tired, but happy that I wouldn't need a C-section after all. My doctor put me on a pitocin drip, which would speed up the labor, explaining we must get the baby out as soon as possible or the baby could flip again.

After a couple of hours, the epidural wore off and I could feel my legs again. For me, feeling the contractions was easier than not feeling my legs. My doctor came in at about 1:00 a.m. and did an internal check. It hurt a lot and then — I couldn't believe it — I realized he had broken my waters! I trusted that he knew what he was doing but did wish he had told me first. He informed me that I was five centimeters dilated and ordered the pitocin drip raised.

I was now receiving the highest dose of pitocin prescribable. The contractions were very strong and were getting longer. I was very tired and weak. I couldn't move around much because I was connected to a monitor. The hours passed slowly. I tried to practice all the breathing I'd learned. I ended up just taking deep breaths through every contraction.

At five o'clock I was still at five centimeters. I was getting discouraged; I couldn't go on much longer. At eight o'clock the doctor returned, but now the contractions were coming very quickly, hard, and long. He checked me and told me my baby could be out in forty-five minutes — in ten minutes I'd be pushing. Finally. It was really happening.

I started feeling pressure. I called the nurse in a panic. All of a sudden I remembered I was a GBS carrier.* I hadn't told them, not expecting to be giving birth there. The nurse ran to get medication to hook up to my IV. All the while I was feeling more and more pressure. My doctor came running in. "Don't push. Breathe with me," he said, so we panted together for about ten minutes until it was safe to start pushing. Enough time had passed for the antibiotic to reach the baby.

Pushing was hard work, but I was excited. At first I told the doctor, "I don't know how!" He calmly coached me along. One push...two pushes...I was running out of strength. Then I said, "Forget it. I can't anymore." The doctor took my hand and put it on my baby's head — soft hair! The head was there! With renewed energy, I pushed a few more times, and he was in my arms, this small, precious little baby boy of mine. Hard work but worth every minute.

---

* GBS (beta-hemolytic streptococcus, known as beta-strep or group B strep) is an organism that is found in the birth canal of up to 25 percent of birthing mothers. Up to 8,000 babies contract strep at birth, with about 800 dying in the U.S. each year. Of those that survive there are serious long-term complications. Therefore women who test positive must take an antibiotic during labor (Finkelstein, *B'Sha'ah Tovah* [Feldheim Publishers, 2001], p. 30).

Birth Center Birth

Susan Lewis

Puff, puff, pant. Puff, puff, pant. Memorize the breathing patterns. Remember to look at the clock. Focus on someone's face, on an object in the room, anything but the pain, anything but what's happening. Just keep your mind off it, and sooner or later it will pass.

It was the birth of my first child. The year was 1978. I labored on a hard bed in a cold room all by myself, lying on my back, wishing someone would at least hold my hand — a nurse, an orderly, anyone! But there I was, all by myself.

The doctor came in after a few hours and decided things weren't going quickly enough — as if four hours for a first birth was too long! Without any sort of explanation, he called for forceps, performed an episiotomy, and the birth was over. Then they took my baby and kept her behind glass in the nursery for three days, only letting me have her every three hours to feed her. I stood in front of the glass looking at her for hours, tears running down my cheeks.

Birth number 2: I was not having *that* experience again, so I opted for a certified nurse-midwife and a home birth — simple, private, in an environment where I felt comfortable and had a say in what would happen. Just us and the miracle of birth. Everything the way I wanted. And that's how it was.

Birth number 3 came when I was forty, and every doctor was calling me "high risk." I always ate well, exercised, and had no medical problems. My husband was nervous about having the baby at home, and I respected his feelings. So we compromised and met somewhere in the middle: the Baltimore Birth Center, five minutes from our home and five minutes from the hospital.

It was a place that had medical facilities in case a problem arose, but also a place where our preferences for the birth would be respected. The nurse-midwives there were used to working with religious ladies and were familiar with the halachos connected with childbirth. They were warm and compassionate, and their attitude toward birth was the same as mine: Hashem made my body capable of giving birth to this baby all by itself, if allowed to do the job without unnecessary intervention.

I continued eating wholesome foods, had a daily brisk walk, went to prenatal exercise classes twice a week, and checked for fetal movements daily. I took my responsibilities seriously. My children were many years apart, so I had the luxury to take extra good care of myself. Even though I worked, I had more time than most women.

All the way through the pregnancy I had a feeling this baby would be born on Shabbos. I was due on Yom Kippur, which, even though it is *the* Shabbos, didn't fall on Shabbos that year.

Birth Center Birth

What I didn't anticipate was that she would be born on Shabbos Rosh HaShanah, a three-day *yom tov* that year. But there we were, sitting at the table on Rosh HaShanah night, my husband trying to make Kiddush between contractions (how that made us laugh!), my labor coach, Susan, an Orthodox woman and my dear friend, helping to serve the meal. It was beautiful to think that our baby would be born on such a holy day. The words of the *machzor* echoed in my mind: "*Hayom haras olam...*" Today is the day of the conception of the world. It would also be the day of the birth of a whole new little world — my child.

After the *yom tov* meal, we sat together in the living room, waiting for the labor to progress. Susan worked with me gently, relaxing me, reminding not to think of the contractions as pain but as discomfort. She helped me accept the discomfort instead of fighting it or running from it.

I surrendered myself to the process of birth. Reminding me that every contraction was one step closer to having my baby at last, Susan helped me with the relaxation exercises we had practiced in the summer. As the labor progressed, I withdrew further into myself, going into a semi-meditative state. Instead of tuning out, I was tuning in. What was going on inside was the most important thing in the world — at least, in my world.

By midnight it became obvious that I was close to transition. I was having trouble relaxing, started to panic, and threw up my dinner. We decided to get going.

When we arrived at the birth center, it was so quiet, so completely peaceful. Susan and I were alone with the two midwives. We women were going to do our special work of helping the baby come into the world. There were no intrusive residents coming to examine me during contractions, none of the hustle and bustle of a hospital. The midwives were there only to be with me, for support and safety, monitoring my baby and taking my vital signs between contractions when I was ready. A nurse waited in another room for when the midwives would need an extra pair of hands. My husband waited in a room down the hall, saying *tehillim* and wearing a path in the rug from pacing.

The first thing the midwives did was let me relax in the Jacuzzi, but after a while it wasn't helping anymore, so they moved me to the shower. That helped for a little while, until I felt some pressure. I moved onto a birth stool in the warm, comfortable bedroom, with Susan right there with me and the midwives working quietly around me in the half-darkened room. All we could hear was the quiet beating of my baby's heart while they monitored it with a handheld device. The Shechinah was in that room, waiting for a new *Yiddishe neshamah* to come into the world.

When Menucha was born, I was able to hold her right away while the nurse and one of the midwives did the necessary examinations. Then they took her to wipe her down and swaddle her warmly before bringing her back to me. Finally we were moved to a queen-sized bed. There we were, the two of us snuggled up together while she latched on.

After a while, my husband came into the room and sat, holding her in the rocking chair, gazing at her, and singing to her till it was time to go daven. Little did I know he would daven at sunrise, then go to every shul in town to tell everyone we knew about our little miracle.

Menucha is seven years old now, and I still remember with amazement the beauty of her birth and the quality support and care I received at the Baltimore Birth Center, which helped make it such a positive memorable experience. We live in Jerusalem now, but when we go back to the States, I take her back to where she got her start to share the affection I have for the place and the midwives. When she was around three years old, I took her to meet Eileen, the midwife who had delivered her. Eileen looked down at her and said, "I remember you when you were so little." Menucha looked up at her and said firmly, "Well, I growed!"

A Beacon in the Fog

S. Bloom

The year was 1953, in November. I hadn't been feeling well all day, so I stayed home, not doing very much. In the late afternoon I realized my unusual feelings were due to labor having started. The pains were really becoming regular now. I called my gynecologist, who said I could stay home longer. (My first birth had taken three days, and I had been sent home in-between.)

When we realized things were picking up, we decided to get a move on. My husband grabbed my not yet two-year-old daughter to take with us since we had absolutely no one to leave her with. We had recently moved to Far Rockaway and barely knew anyone. Since we had to get to Beth Israel Hospital in Manhattan, my husband started driving quickly.

On top of all the anxiety, it was a drizzly, foggy night. My husband tried not to go too quickly over the Williamsburg Bridge, but my screams of panic and my daughter's cries at seeing her mommy like this really shook him up. He even asked a policeman to help, but his only offer of assistance was to tell us to drive slowly and carefully.

Soon after, I shouted, "I am giving birth!"

Just as we crossed over the bridge, the car stalled. In my husband's panic, he couldn't get it started. I screamed, "Don't stop here. Oh, it's dead!" My husband thought I meant the baby when I was talking about the car. He was beside himself.

Suddenly he saw a young man walking down the sidewalk in our direction, carrying a bag. "We need help," my husband called out to him.

Was this Eliyahu HaNavi? We needed help, but from a man? How could he possibly help me? What should I ask him to do — calm my daughter? Catch the baby? The five seconds it took the young man to reach us felt like hours.

My husband said, "Please help us. My wife is having a baby in the car."

"I am an obstetrician," he answered, almost putting my husband into shock.

He delivered the baby, wrapping it in his new coat. My husband insisted that he would pay for the coat. The man refused. He said, "Although I am Jewish, I am not a religious man, but this is God's baby."

My husband got the car started again by simply turning the key. A reason was never discovered as to why it stalled in the first place.

On the way to the hospital, the young doctor told us how he "happened" to be there.

He was a resident obstetrician at Beth Israel Hospital. Even though this was his day off, he decided to go to the hospital and sleep over since he was starting early in the morning. His mother asked him, "Why so early?" He said, "I just feel like I have to go now, even in this crazy weather." She tried to convince him to stay home, but he felt like he needed to walk, so he left.

For years to come, he sent birthday cards, never forgetting our son's birthday.

Jacuzzi Birth

Debbie Sassen

The birth of my fifth child reminded me, initially, of my third. The end, however, was amazing and beautiful — dramatically different and never to be repeated again.

Labor started with a show, followed about half a day later with the onset of regular contractions. I was sure "this was it," and I started getting excited. By late evening, however, contractions had stopped completely, and I went to sleep a bit disappointed. I had a keen sense of déjà vu.

The next morning I decided that it was time to stop working, hopeful that perhaps today was going to be the day. I called my boss, informing her that I was officially starting my maternity leave.

I went about my daily business — davening, errands, and even a bris (soon by me, I hoped). I was vaguely aware that I was having contractions.

At around 3 p.m. I called my labor coach and told her the contractions were regular — about every ten minutes. I started to get myself organized, pack my bag, and get supper ready for the family. My labor coach phoned me back at around 6 p.m. to see how I was doing. I was giving the kids dinner. Contractions had stopped, and I was getting really frustrated. "I don't think this baby is ever going to come out," I told her.

Shortly thereafter my husband came home from work, and I went out for a walk. I was very edgy and walked very quickly. (I had kept up walking throughout the pregnancy, so I had no problem doing a "power walk" at this point — of course, that's the way it seemed to me, but considering that I was nine months pregnant, I could have been walking at a snail's pace.) I was aware that my stomach was contracting, but I walked through the contractions, not heeding the pain. After about an hour or so, I came home. I went to my bedroom to focus my thoughts and, admittedly, to avoid bedtime.

About a half-hour later, while lying in bed, I had a super-strong contraction that took my breath away and left me no doubt that I was in active labor. I jumped out of bed.

My husband was putting our two-year-old to sleep, and, in spite of the pain, I went to take over and rock with him in the rocking chair, aware that tomorrow I wouldn't be there for him and that he would no longer be my baby. After he fell asleep, I called my labor coach to tell her we were on the way to the hospital.

I'm always excited, but a bit anxious when entering the hospital. I want to know where I'm holding, but I don't want to be disappointed. With my third and fourth babies, I arrived at the hospital at about eight centimeters. So I was a bit disappointed when the midwife told me I was only six centimeters dilated.

The midwife hooked me up to the monitor. I don't like this part of the routine very much. I like being upright and even squat through contractions. I've read it really helps the baby move through the birth canal. I tried to focus on my contractions and breathe through them. My labor coach massaged my feet while I was hooked to the monitor, which helped me relax.

After monitoring the baby, the midwife suggested I go into the Jacuzzi located in the birthing room at the end of the hall. By the time my assistant and I gathered our belongings and filled the Jacuzzi, an hour had passed since I had been checked. While dropping the fragrant aromatherapy oils into the water, my assistant advised me to be aware of any pressure. I would naturally feel more buoyant while being immersed in the water.

My senses were filled with lavender, music, and massage (by my assistant). I was very relaxed, although a bit weary. I tried to focus my thoughts on my soon-to-be-born baby.

Then it came — the pressure my assistant warned me about. "I think I feel pressure," I told her.

"How strong?" she asked.

"Very strong." I took a deep breath.

"Let's go. You're coming out," said my assistant.

I didn't have time to respond. I was so relaxed that my body just took over. I shifted my position so that I was sitting on my knees. I took a deep breath, bore down, and pushed.

"The head! It's the head!" I screamed.

My assistant looked down to see the head emerging, and she took a spin toward the door to call the midwife.

"The baby is coming out in the water!" she cried.

As she turned to assist me, there was the experience that I would never have thought possible — another push and my baby just slipped out into the water. "It's a boy!"

I was ecstatic. I gently lifted him out of the water, holding him close till the midwife arrived. I remember thinking, *He's so purple*. Later I learned this was because he had been born into a water-filled environment rather than oxygen. Since he was still attached to me through the umbilical cord, this was normal and safe, I was told.

The midwife arrived and cut the cord. I was gently assisted out of the Jacuzzi to finish the third stage of delivery and nurse the baby. It was a beautiful birth. I had birthed my baby completely and totally by myself.

> *Editor's note*: A bath or Jacuzzi should be kept at 98 degrees Fahrenheit or lower. It may slow down contractions in early labor; however, in active labor, it can relax a woman and open her up as the contractions continue but are felt much less. Most medical authorities agree that if the membranes are intact, baths are an effective and safe means of laboring. More research is being done on the safety of baths if the amniotic membranes are not intact.

The Next Best Thing

Rochel Tova

September 5. That's the day the doctor said was my due date. *How many people really give birth on their due date?* I thought. Moshe and I had gotten married only two months ago, so we were still enjoying being *chasan* and *kallah*, and I was completing my speech therapy training. With all this I didn't focus much on the birth — that was months away.

The pregnancy went quicker than I thought it would. We went to my mom's for Pesach and continued the year learning and going to friends' *chasunah*s.

My doctor was a great lady as well as a good doctor. If I needed an extra couple of minutes during my routine visit, she gave it to me. The pregnancy was going well. I barely had morning sickness and felt pretty good.

Then it happened. The middle-of-the-night ache in the lower back my friends told me about. Actually, it spread toward my stomach, and although they started at twenty-minute intervals, they proceeded quickly to being ten minutes apart. At 8 a.m. they were four, sometimes six, minutes apart, and I felt I wanted to be checked. I went to the hospital, and the nurse there said I was already four centimeters dilated and 80 percent effaced, but since it was a first birth, I could continue laboring at home for a few hours. The baby was doing fine on the monitor, so we left.

At 11 a.m. and again at 2 p.m. we returned. There was some progress in effacement, but still four centimeters in dilation. The contractions were still erratic, and the monitor was fine, so we went back home. Unfortunately sleep was beyond us. What was the next best thing? I rested in a warm bath. I called a childbirth educator, who suggested I lie in a different position to see if that might speed up the labor. I davened.

At 8 p.m. we asked to be checked again, and believe it or not, we were allowed to go home one more time. I was completely effaced but the same four centimeters open. I wasn't interested in pain medication so my doctor said I could go home and try to get some sleep. I sat in a warm bath, did my breathing, and called my childbirth educator again to ask for some more position ideas. She suggested that the baby might not be in an optimal position. I did some lunging to the side, some crazy side movements. This was the next best thing, and I was willing to try anything.

When I returned to the hospital once again, I was desperate. If I hadn't progressed, I knew I would break down. The contractions were seven to ten minutes apart, and my husband was also starting to falter.

Now it was midnight. I was four to five centimeters open (maybe). I cried. I just couldn't anymore. The next best thing: everyone decided that Demerol would help me sleep, perhaps relaxing me enough to open up.

By 3 a.m. when there was still no progress, my doctor suggested pitocin. I suppose that was the next best thing, and I accepted it gladly. I tried to do my breathing and visualization, dozing in-between, but by eight in the morning, even with the pitocin dose increased, I was dilated only five centimeters. There was no question I would have an epidural. At noon, even the top-up of the epidural had little effect, so the doctor gave me a spinal combination. I still don't know what that is, but it worked. My doctor was the *shaliach* I had really needed. She had such patience. When I was eight centimeters open, she said, "As long as the baby is doing fine, we can wait longer." It was obvious we were trying to avoid a cesarean even though no one said it outright. By 1:30 p.m. having been on the highest dose of pitocin she would give, I opened to ten centimeters, but the baby's head was still high.

Another hour with no progression — no matter how I turned my body, the head didn't come down. At 2:45, I was prepped for a cesarean, the next best thing.

So, on September 7, my eight-pound baby was born, with a molded head. The doctor explained to me the condition called cephalopelvic disproportion — when the baby's head is too big for the mother's pelvis. She said it didn't mean I can't ever have a normal birth. I was also happy when she told me that having opened up to ten can make the next birth easier. I accepted the fact that I did all I could and this wasn't all in vain.

I feel so great knowing that at each hurdle I thought, *Okay, Hashem, I see what I want isn't exactly what you have in mind for me.* Then I went on to the next best thing.

Postpartum's Gaping Black Hole

Denise Blumberg

My first struggle with postpartum depression occurred when I was still living in the United States with my husband and three kids. I was thirty-three years old and had for the previous six years been working on my Ph.D. A mere two weeks after submitting the final draft of my thesis, I gave birth to a healthy, 8-pound baby girl. She was born at home, by choice, and I was surrounded by friends and caregivers.

The period immediately following her birth was exhilarating. My Ph.D. came through during Sukkos, which added to an already festive *yom tov*. Life was normal and happy. I was busy with the kids, tending to my family's needs, the house, going back to aerobics classes — all the normal functions of daily living.

I was not prepared for the turmoil that awaited me some four months afterward. I had not experienced any postpartum reaction with any of my three previous babies; I didn't recognize it when it began.

At first, I simply felt down. The feelings of my afterbirth exhilaration faded and left me hanging somewhere between birth and life. Then I began to lose enthusiasm for my usual interests and found myself milling around the house with the sense of having nothing to do.

As the weeks progressed, this intensified into a deep and terrifying feeling that I had nothing to do with my days, nothing to do with my life. A shroud of meaninglessness seemed to seep up from the depths of the earth and envelop my body. A gaping black hole began somewhere in my throat and ballooned when it reached my stomach. It made me physically nauseous. Although I lost my appetite and could barely taste the food, I ate a lot, trying to fill the ever-widening void within.

My brain was very detached from all of this. It was aware that my situation was growing worse. But for once, there was nothing my intellect could do to help me. Whatever was happening to me was not cognitive.

My ability to cope with the kids and the house deteriorated, which led to panic and despair. I feared that this was a form of insanity.

In normal circumstances, we take coping for granted, and we don't realize the inner strength that goes into just coping. When postnatal depression descends like a black cloud, there's no such thing as coping. The word itself drops out of one's vocabulary as if it never existed.

The thought of shopping overwhelmed me with anxiety. The idea of juggling the demands of the kids threw me into a series of severe heart palpitations. I still had no idea what was happening to me. Had I not had a full-time nanny, I think I would have been out of my mind with fear.

The actual details of my life at that time are blurred. I remember more the feelings, the sensations and terrors. When I woke in the morning, the gnawing black hole inside almost devoured me. I could barely drag myself from the bed. Making a cup of coffee was unthinkable.

Getting dressed was fraught with so many choices, I was torn apart by panic. Much better not to get dressed. Ever.

I was unable to perform the most minor tasks. Preparing a simple meal — toast and butter — was an enormous burden I could not undertake for anything in the world. An hour or so before the kids would come back from school I would feel a surge of panic in my throat, making breathing difficult. Something inside kept on screaming, "You can't cope with this! You'll never manage the demands!" And I didn't. Every time a child asked for something as minor as an apple, it felt like he was asking for a 747 jumbo jet.

The daily battles with the toddler about getting dressed made me feel as if I was in the middle of a war zone, as if I was about to be struck by a bomb. And indeed, I was far more terrified then than I have ever been during the situation here in Israel. I found the terror within much more devastating than the terror without; for I breathed it all the time — or, rather, it breathed me. I was its desperate slave. And those inner sensations threatened to consume me completely.

I just left everything to the nanny. (We lived then in the United States and were luckily able to afford one.) She fed the kids. She bathed them. She put them to bed when my husband wasn't at home. I don't remember who did the shopping — for sure it wasn't me.

I still had no idea what was happening to me. I only knew that the worst thing in the world was to be conscious, because what I craved more than anything was the bliss of unconsciousness. I didn't want to know I was alive because I was where Hell was and Hell was where I was, and we were as deformed in our bonds as Siamese twins. If I wanted anyone at all in this purgatory, it was the baby, and the only thing I wanted to do was to coil myself around her in bed, go to sleep, and never wake up.

The Turning Point

The turning point happened one morning. I was sitting on my bed, rocking backward and forward, hugging a cushion to my chest as if it was a life-support machine. My husband came into the room, and I remember bursting out, "What is the matter with me?"

"You need to see a doctor."

My husband's reply was in itself a great blessing. Many husbands are utterly confused by this sudden change in their wives, and the idea of her seeing a psychiatrist or taking pills only intensifies their fear.

My doctor was a highly sensitive woman who specialized in women's issues. She immediately diagnosed postpartum depression, and this gave me the light of hope. If there was a name to what I was experiencing, perhaps there was also a cure.

This light of hope enabled my husband to revolutionize. Before I was diagnosed, he felt completely helpless and unable to understand what I was experiencing. Once he knew that there was something clinically, medically the matter with me, he completely took over my role, cooking and dealing with the needs of the kids.

I was again very blessed. What might have happened had he been bitter or resentful? What if he'd been angry at suddenly finding himself the captain of a sinking ship?

My doctor advised me to see a psychiatrist, who prescribed antidepressant medication, which he said would take a few weeks to kick in. I was deathly afraid of pills, having no idea what this kind of drug would do to me. I was terrified of being out of control. But I was so terribly out of control anyway that I simply had no choice.

This medication was the difference between heaven and hell. I felt like an entirely new person.

Aliyah and More Kids

When my fifth child was born three years later, there was no recurrence whatsoever of postnatal depression, and I truly believed I was free forever of what I thought had been a one-time occurrence.

Almost two years after making aliyah, I gave birth to a perfectly healthy baby — but who weighed just over three pounds. Unlike the uneventful pregnancy of my previous postpartum baby, this pregnancy had been fraught with anxieties. There had been questions about the health of the baby from early on, and I didn't know what would be with her.

The birth was traumatic, and she was separated from me. I was barely allowed to hold her, and I was certainly not allowed to nurse her. She was placed in an incubator for about two weeks in a hospital in the greater Tel Aviv area, and the daily trips to see her from Jerusalem involved a three-hour excursion.

During those weeks I was expressing milk at two-hourly intervals, around the clock, in a desperate attempt to keep my milk and be able to nurse her. By the time we brought home this tiny little baby, I was completely exhausted and utterly overwhelmed.

To my absolute horror, I began to experience those

same old terrible feelings. The same nausea, the same feelings of emptiness and panic, the gaping black hole, and the desperate imaginings of how I was ever going to cope.

But this time there was no nanny. No one to take the kids, no one to make supper, no one to hold the baby — *no one*.

My husband had professional commitments. He couldn't simply stay home and nurse me, which was exactly what I needed. This time, it didn't help him to know the name and condition of what I was going through.

My husband's initial reaction expressed the stark difference between my postpartum depression in America and this new, Israeli experience. Fraught with anxiety, he told me that he never wanted to have more children because he couldn't cope with what I go through when I have a baby. And this from someone who always said he could manage with ten children. The sense of isolation and aloneness made him feel that now everything was on his shoulders and he felt completely overburdened and unable to face that task.

But this time there was Nitza, a nonprofit support network for women experiencing postpartum depression, which I had heard about through a friend who had been helped by them.

I cannot overemphasize the importance of quality support after birth. Hormones are in an uproar, sometimes causing extreme outbursts of anger or tears. Because a new baby brings so much excitement and joy, the fact that women may also be very vulnerable at this time is something often not understood. From the moment I heard Chana's voice on the phone, I knew that I wasn't alone. I was almost light-headed with relief knowing that she understood, that she had a network of support people in various roles pulling together to help me in the way that I needed help.

I was struck by the selflessness underlying the organization. Nothing was imposed upon me; I didn't have to do anything I didn't want to do or didn't feel was right for me. Nitza's only concern was to address my needs.

Because I had been through postnatal depression before, I was very aware of my needs. Nitza's director of client services phoned me twice a day, every day. I have no recollection of what we spoke about, but the fact that she cared enough just to phone allowed me to integrate the emotional support I so desperately needed. A Nitza volunteer counselor was in constant contact, listening to me, sharing my pain, and allowing me to feel normal and human within my desolation. And always, there was the knowledge of professionals behind the scenes, liasing, thinking, advising, cushioning.

As per my request, Nitza organized natural medication through a homeopathic practitioner, which helped enormously to calm my anxiety. Meals were organized on an extended basis to remove the pressure of taking care of my family. Young girls were brought in to look after the other children when I needed to rest, and others were recruited to hold the baby when I needed to spend time with the older kids. And eventually, Nitza found in-house help for as long as I needed it. They had taken care of my needs, preventing me from plunging again into the pit of postpartum depression.

If women experience trauma that is overwhelmingly intense, as I had in my first confrontation with this syndrome, conventional medication may well be a matter of life and death. The gentle effects of my homeopaths' remedies may not be sufficiently aggressive to deal with a condition that is indeed marriage-threatening, kids-threatening — life-threatening. In His great kindness, the Almighty brought Nitza to me, to my husband, and to my children. I was amazed by the lengths to which these women were prepared to go just to help. With the personal emotional support and the practical help in the house that they organized, my spirits began to lift almost immediately, for I knew I was not alone and didn't have to cope on my own. Together, we had weathered an ominous storm.

> This article was reprinted with permission from the Aish.com Web site.
>
> Nitza: The Jerusalem Postpartum Support Network was founded in 1997 to provide support to women and their families suffering from postpartum illness, including postpartum depression, psychosis, and mania. Nitza is currently the only organization in Israel providing a full spectrum of services meeting the unique needs of those suffering postpartum illness.

Snowstorm over Jerusalem

Michal Gutman

My due date came and went. They call it EDD — "estimated" due date. I suppose that's to calm down women like me who can get nervous as the day approaches. I was only one day over, but it may as well have been two weeks. As it was, when we were approaching Shabbos the week before, I got edgy, talkative, and kept questioning our plan of action if it were to happen on Shabbos.

To add to my anxiety, for the first time in ten years the weatherman was predicting a snowstorm. Being a New Yorker, I wasn't too concerned at first. Then, one of my neighbors, who was here during the last snowstorm, starting telling me how it had affected the city. Jerusalem was not only immobilized; it was downright paralyzed. There were a few crazy drivers who had tried to get to their destinations only to get stuck before they arrived.

I live in an area in the northern part of Jerusalem

about four miles from the nearest hospital. That's fairly close, considering most people travel from a half-hour to an hour to get to the place they are giving birth. But I had two things going against me.

The first was the storm, and the second that this was my second birth. Most first births take much longer than second births. At least, that's what the books said. Unless the circumstances are very unusual, by the time those hard contractions that had us at five centimeters during the first birth come, one could be fully dilated!

Monday evening came. I wasn't sure the aches I was experiencing were Braxton-Hicks, real contractions, or indigestion. I was distracted while giving my husband dinner, and neither of us was paying much attention to the weather.

As the evening progressed, we started timing the (now obvious) contractions. I was about to pack my bag but decided to put up another load of wash and do the supper dishes. Don't most women do that? I also decided to wait to call my labor coach because my husband and I wanted to go through this stage together. At my first birth, my mom was with my husband and I, so my husband felt a bit left out. I had decided I would include him more this time.

As contractions became more intense, Mordechai began packing a bag. I couldn't find the list I had prepared, which made us a bit more frazzled. I had known we would have time during labor so why not wait to pack a bag? Wouldn't it keep us occupied when the time came?

I called my labor coach at 11 p.m. She saw how quickly the snowstorm was progressing and said we should call a cab right away and finish packing while he was on the way. We agreed. The only thing we had to do was go get a yeshivah student to watch our sleeping baby. The yeshivah was one long block away, and my labor coach a block beyond that. When the coach called back a half-hour later and found out we hadn't brought the student yet, she said she would arrange the cab in the meantime. Now the contractions were three minutes apart.

We called five cab companies; no one was willing to come so far. My labor coach went out to try to hail one. At this point, nothing was in the streets except plows being used as snow shovels. She turned back to phone for an ambulance when, driving up the road from a deserted area of our community, was a van taxi with no sign in the window. She flagged him down and asked him if he would drive to the hospital. He agreed, and she ran back into her house, called me, grabbed her bag, and gave the driver directions. When they arrived at my house, the list had still not been found and my bag still not packed, but she said, "We have to leave *now*." We slowly made our way out of the house as my husband said goodbye to my mom, whom we had called to ask her to daven for me.

I couldn't even enjoy the snow, because the pressure was so great by then that my coach had me on all fours with my head down. She didn't want more pressure than the contractions were already causing. This position countered gravity and would give me more time.

When we arrived at the hospital, I insisted on walking to the delivery room. The midwife was not pleased when I told her I had forgotten my card with the prenatal information and my registration papers. It was on the list that I never found.

I said, "If I am less than eight centimeters, I am going to go crazy." The orange aromatherapy scent my coach had prepared for me and her firm touch helped me focus. When the midwife told me I was ten centimeters I could have screamed for joy.

When my beautiful daughter entered the world, I only remembered asking over and over if she had ten fingers and ten toes. Hearing my mom's happiness when she heard that there was finally a granddaughter after five grandsons enhanced the thrill. She would be at the store first thing in the morning to buy anything pink. In the meantime, I would hold my new baby watching the quiet midnight snow continue to cover the treetops from the huge sixth-floor window.

It's a Girl!

Batya Jacobs

I first realized it at the hospital. Those uncomfortable aches I was having that gradually become pains and finally turn into pressure meant birth was imminent. I had just finished a routine antenatal visit. "You should have this baby within two weeks" was the verdict. Two weeks, my foot! This baby was already on its way!

I wanted to start the birth from home. I wanted to pack my hospital bag, explain to my children that I was going to get the baby, and give them all big kisses. I wanted to give my youngest his last baby cuddle. Then I could go back to the hospital and give birth. So I went home, driven along the bumpy, twisting road to my little half-horse settlement, rather a long half-hour ride from Yerushalayim. Yerushalayim, dreamed of by my ancestors, prayed for day by day, lost for so long, now ours again. Yerushalayim — where better to bring forth the next generation?

I arrived home, the nagging contractions coming and going — some strong, some little tickles. I sat down in my rocking chair, rhythmically rocking myself through contractions. Baby and I were lulled by the slow backward and forward motion, while my body was relentlessly ending our total physical togetherness.

I had to pack my bag. I prepared the carriage that would serve as the baby's bed in the early weeks. I put the pink and blue blanket on top — you never know what you might have, and this blanket would serve for a boy or a girl.

The contractions worsened as I walked around and calmed down a bit when I sat. *This is it*, I thought. *These contractions really mean business.*

I rang my labor coach. For the first few births, I had taken my husband with me. He didn't like the experience. His wife was in discomfort, and he didn't know what to do there anyway. I happened upon a friendship with a lady who was a labor coach, so I took her along as a kind of cheerleader, someone who was exclusively on my side. She'd given birth many times and knew just how I might be feeling. So I phoned her.

"Fancy a trip to Yerushalayim?" I asked.

"I'll just find myself a babysitter, and I'll be right over," she replied.

We took the birth kit, just in case. I told the kids that their father would be home from work soon. With a noisy farewell to my six sons, we left to deliver baby number seven.

This birth was going to be different. The hospital where I was going had asked me to include a "birth plan" when I registered. I had planned a birth with the minimum of interference and the maximum of encouragement. After all, how many times do you give birth in a lifetime? Birthing should be a positive experience — something to look back on with a smile on your face. I wanted to feel relaxed and glowing with accomplishment when this baby and I would first meet. I wanted to push my baby out to the tune of smiling, enthusiastic encouragement as that day-to-day miracle known as birth happened.

We traveled, my labor coach and I, in her old jalopy. We twisted and turned, bumped and climbed and climbed and climbed up to Yerushalayim. During the journey I thought about my children, my boys. The oldest was just thirteen, bar mitzvah, a fully responsible adult Jew. My youngest, a chatterbox, a smiley, rambunctious two-year-old. My baby. Who would put him to bed tonight? I wiped a tear from my eye. *Now come on,* I thought to myself, *let's not get morose!*

"Remember to get it right again!" all the boys had said. "And if you get it wrong, swap her for a boy. Nobody will notice." My boys, bless their cotton socks.

The tears streamed down my face. *It must be transition.* Transition from getting ready to give birth to the actual process of birthing. Ladies "go funny" in transition. They normally just want to forget the whole thing and go home. *Oh, well, it's too late now.*

We arrived at the hospital. We were checked in. The contractions were long and hard, so I sang my song, "Be Kind to Your Web-Footed Friend," a silly song I had chosen so many years ago at the psychoprophelaxis class at the Birmingham Maternity Hospital.

"Look at her! She's singing!"

One by one, the staff came in to see this odd scene. She's singing her way through her labor. What else is there to do? Singing keeps you breathing, keeps your mind off the pain, keeps you and your dumbfounded audience happy until you need to push. Push. That word takes on another meaning once you've had your first baby. When can I push, am I ready to push, go ahead push, come on, just one more push. From the very first twinge of labor, that's what you wait for — "PUSH!"

My midwife had just delivered a huge baby who had gotten stuck by his shoulders. It's not easy to handle such a birth, but with the help of a doctor, the baby made a successful and raucous entrance to this world. My midwife was nervous about a repeat performance.

"This baby might be a big one," she said to me. "If the head is big, I shall lower your bed so you are lying down."

The delivery bed had been converted into a chair so I could give birth sitting up. Above my head a mirror had been carefully place so I could see the whole process should I wish, and if I didn't want to see all of it, then perhaps I might just watch the moment of entry.

My midwife said that magic word. *This is it*, I thought. PUSH, here we go, PUSH, I'm starting to PUSH. The baby's head must have been big because suddenly my bed floated its way backward. I shut my eyes. *This isn't happening to me.* I braced myself. Okay, forget about all that sermonizing on enjoyable birthing, the atmosphere, the noninterference, the natural childbirth — let me just get this baby *out*! The bed finished its journey, I finished my pushing, and the hard part known as "crowning" had been achieved.

"Come on, one more push, that's a girl, just one more like that, I know you can do it, hold that push, more, more, more, *you did it*!"

"It's a girl!"

I had dreamed of this happening so many times. I had imagined all the possible things I might say, all the different ways it might happen — from the dramatic birth in the ambulance to the mundane birth in the hospital. Each version had me pontificating on the miracle, sometimes witty, sometimes profound, but always to the point, always fitting for the exclusivity of the moment. When it actually happened, though, I wasn't expecting it.

"But she looks just like all the boys!" I said.

"What did you expect, a ponytail and ribbons?" commented my labor coach.

I was taken up to the maternity ward. The nurses greeted me with a *mazel tov*. I don't remember if the ward nurses said congratulations when I arrived at the ward after my births in England. *Mazel tov* is such a warm, sincere greeting, a simple marketplace sharing of my joy. These people, my people, really care.

The *mohel*, the man trained to perform ritual circumcision, made his morning rounds. As usual, he said a general *mazel tov* and then asked each occupant, "Boy or girl?" If the answer was "boy," he enthused and made sure you had a reliable *mohel* for the circumcision. If you said "girl," he'd mutter something roughly translated as "Hard luck. Better luck next time!" *I've done my bit for boys*, I thought, *and no doubt I'll "get it right" for my boys next time*. But now I deserve a completely unreserved "Well done!" for my little girl.

I took her home. No, I didn't even try to swap her. Gradually it hit me that I really had a girl. That first Friday night there was no traditional gathering to welcome a new Jewish boy to the world. On the eighth day there was no circumcision. All my neighbors lent me their pink baby clothes. My husband couldn't voice disappointment. Feminine cunning had no doubt helped my daughter to make her appearance coincide with her father's birthday. I fetched out a poem I'd once written to a friend who had had a girl after two boys. I read it to the boys to show my empathy.

It's a Girl!

A girl, oh, dear, a girl
Just think of all the dollies
With the doll clothes in our car box
And the doll's pram with our lorries

A girl, oh, dear, a girl
Just think of all her dresses
Piles of pink all over our wardrobe
And another "*Yekke*" about messes

A girl, oh, dear, a girl
Just think of all that squealing
When we put tadpoles in her perfume
And hang spiders from the ceiling

A girl, oh, dear, a girl
We suppose we wish you joy
Have a pink thing for her collection
And next time — do have a boy!

I made cake for the *kiddush*. One was a huge rectangle lined with roses. In the middle was a doll cake with a flowing pink ball dress — my little princess.

I love my boys, all eight of them (yes, another two were born), but it's so much fun to have a girl!

Afterword

I hope these stories have been enjoyable and provided *chizuk*. I purposely did not incorporate stories with disappointing endings. But those are also part of God's plan, and in a future book I would like to include these in a chapter called "A Different Type of *Chizuk*."

I also do not want anyone to feel guilty if, due to personal reasons, past history, or a difficult labor, their birth experience did not go as they had hoped. With the support of a husband, caregiver, and *rav* the right decision for your circumstances can be made. Once made, do not compare yourself to others, and again, do not feel guilty.

If anyone is interested in sharing a story that will provide laughter, inspiration, comfort, and insights, please send your story by e-mail: emgee@netvision.net.il or snail mail: PO Box 27613, Neve Yaakov, Jerusalem, Israel.

Glossary

bar mitzvah — Ceremony to mark a boy turning thirteen, when he becomes obligated in the commandments.

baruch Hashem — Thank God.

bitachon — Trust in God.

bris milah — Ritual circumcision performed on the eighth day after the birth of a male child.

challos — Braided bread traditionally eaten on the Sabbath and festivals.

chesed — Kind-heartedness; giving to others.

chizuk — Strengthening; reinforcement.

chuppah — Wedding ceremony.

daven — To pray.

emunah — Religious faith.

Eretz Yisrael — Land of Israel.

erev Shabbos — Sabbath eve.

HaKadosh Baruch Hu — The Holy One, blessed be He.

Haman — Viceroy of Persia, circa 365 C.E., determined to wipe out exiled Jewish communities in the Persian empire. When the Purim story is read, it is traditional to sound noisemakers and stamp feet to symbolize the erasing of his name and memory.

Hashem — God.

hishtadlus — Effort to help oneself.

Kiddush — Sanctification of the Sabbath or a festival by reciting a blessing over a cup of wine; gathering at which this sanctification blessing is recited and food is served.

kollel — Torah institution of full-time study for married men.

kvater — Ceremonial honor accorded at a bris milah, usually to a childless couple.

maggid shiur — Senior teacher in a yeshivah.

mazel tov — "Congratulations"; traditional greeting upon hearing of a joyous event.

megillah — Story of the Purim saga, read publicly on the fourteenth of Adar or the fifteenth in walled cities, such as Jerusalem.

melaveh malkah — Traditional festive meal eaten after the conclusion of Sabbath, on Saturday night.

minyan — Quorum of ten men for the purpose of public prayer.

mishmeres — Group of people who take on saying or learning laws, such as those of forbidden speech, for the benefit of another, be it for good health, a soul mate, or children.

mitzvah — Torah commandment.

mohel — Ritual circumciser.

motza'ei Shabbos — The conclusion of the Sabbath; Saturday night.

nachas — Proud pleasure (in a spiritual or emotional sense).

Glossary

pidyon haben — Ceremony of the redemption of the firstborn son, performed thirty days after birth.

Purim — Festival celebrated on the fourteenth day of Adar (in walled cities such as Jerusalem, on the fifteenth), commemorating the Jews' victory over their enemies wishing to destroy them during the period of the Persian exile.

A freilechen Purim — Happy Purim.

rav — Rabbi.

Rebbe — Head of a chassidic sect.

rosh kollel — Head of a *kollel*.

rosh yeshivah — Head of a yeshivah, high school, or post-high school for boys.

sefer — Book; holy book.

segulah — Spiritual remedy.

seudah — Festive meal.

Shabbos — Sabbath.

shacharis — Morning prayers.

shalom zachar — Festive gathering held on the first Friday night after the birth of a male child.

shiur — Study lesson; lecture; measurement or amount.

shomer Shabbos — Sabbath observant.

shul — Synagogue.

simchah — Joy; joyous occasion.

Sukkos — Festival of Tabernacles, lasting eight days.

Tishah B'Av — Day of mourning on ninth day in the Hebrew month of Av commemorating the destruction of both the first and second Temples in Jerusalem.

tzaddik — Very spiritual people who live their lives connected to God and learning and living His Torah for its sake alone.

vasikin — Earliest possible morning prayer service, usually beginning just before sunrise.

yeshivah — Religious seminary for boys or men.

yemach shemam — Literally, "May their names be eradicated."

yemach shemo v'zichro — "May his name and his memory be eradicated."

yom tov — Jewish traditional festival, usually associated with the three pilgrimage festivals.

zt"l — Acronym for "*zecher tzaddik livrachah* — may the memory of this holy person be blessed."

Glossary of Medical Terms

amniotic fluid — Fluid surrounding the fetus contained in a balloon-type sac.

aromatherapy — Aromatic oils used, in birth, primarily for massage and relaxation.

breech presentation — Presentation in which buttocks or legs are nearest the cervical opening (3 percent of all births).

cervix — Mouth of the uterus.

cesarean section/birth — Birth of a fetus by an incision through the walls of the abdomen and uterus.

crowning — The stage of birth when the top of the fetal head can be seen at the vaginal opening, before delivery.

Demerol — A narcotic introduced through an injection in the thigh muscle or intravenously through the IV line. It causes some women to feel sleepy, only to wake up at the peek of the contraction, relaxing them enough to open up. Others feel out of control, dizzy, and nauseated.

dilation — Stretching of the cervix to 10 centimeters for the baby to pass through.

doula — Professional labor assistant.

effacement — Thinning and shortening of the cervix that occurs during late pregnancy or early labor, measured in percentages.

epidural — Type of regional anesthesia produced by injection of a local anesthetic into the epidural space of the spinal column.

fetal monitor — External, or the more accurate internal, tracking of fetal heart rate and contractions.

forceps — A curved-blade stainless-steel instrument used to assist in delivery of fetus when intervention is necessary.

heparin lock — Plastic cap attached to a thin tube in the forearm keeping a line open into the bloodstream. An IV line for fluids, pitocin (see below), or blood transfusion, can then be connected to this.

HypnoBirthing — A method taught in childbirth education classes that helps the woman maintain control through deep relaxation, to help herself through the process of childbirth.

pitocin — The chemical (synthetic) form of the hormone oxytocin that is released from the posterior pituitary gland to stimulate uterine contraction. It provides harder, more frequent contractions.

placenta — A specialized vascular, disk-shaped organ (similar to the liver) for maternal-fetal oxygen, nutrients, and metabolic exchange.

thrombosis — Clot formation.

transition — The phase late in the first stage of labor in which a woman dilates from 8 to 10 centimeters.

transverse presentation — Presentation in which the fetus lies on the side, horizontally, within the uterus (1 percent occurs in all births, requiring a cesarean).

ultrasound/ultrasonography — Use of high-frequency sound waves for a variety of obstetric diagnoses and scan of the fetus.

waters "breaking" — Term used for when the amniotic fluid starts to leak or actually bursts, an indication that labor will probably start within twenty-four hours.